Learning _through_ play:
Babies, Toddlers and the Foundation Years

Tina Bruce

Hodder & Stoughton
A MEMBER OF THE HODDER HEADLINE GROUP

Dedication

To Elizabeth Bevan Roberts.

A steadfast friend, whose wisdom and gentle humour has sustained me: a catalyst, who quietly but surely helps those working in education to keep going, even when it is tough.

Orders: please contact Bookpoint Ltd, 130 Milton Park, Abingdon, Oxon OX14 4SB. Telephone: (44) 01235 827720, Fax: (44) 01235 400454. Lines are open from 9.00 – 6.00, Monday to Saturday, with a 24 hour message answering service. Email address: orders@bookpoint.co.uk

British Library Cataloguing in Publication Data

A catalogue record for this title is available from The British Library

ISBN 0 340 80152 2

First published 2001

Impression number   10 9 8 7 6 5 4 3 2 1

Year   2005 2004 2003 2002 2001

Typeset by Fakenham Photosetting Limited Fakenham Norfolk

Printed in Italy for Hodder & Stoughton Educational, a division of Hodder Headline Plc, 338 Euston Road, London NW1 3BH.

Contents

Acknowledgements

I should like to thank Tom Bruce, whose unobtrusive photography allowed the play to flow. Much of the text is centred around the photographs and the play which they record.

My thanks to Margery and Peter Rowland for many different kinds of help.

Thank you also to Hannah Bruce, who was my personal assistant during the period of writing the book.

As always, my thanks to Ian Bruce, who is always there for me.

I should like to thank Elisabeth Tribe, Anna Clark and Victoria Foster for their support and help.

Special thanks to the families, and to the parents, children, and staff of Flora Nursery, in Flora Gardens Community Centre, Hammersmith, London (Linda Palmer, Jackie Palmer, Marie Housain, Sabrina Wright, and Michelle Ainsbro), who were so welcoming to Tom and me.

Introduction

······

Aim

This book is designed to help adults who spend time with babies, toddlers and children in their Foundation Years (0–6). The focus is on learning through play. The aim is to help adults develop well-planned play during the first six years of a child's life, and hopefully beyond.

You may wish to read Part 2 only, since Part 1 of the book sets the scene historically, culturally and politically, forming a backdrop to Part 2. Part 2 gives practical ways in which adults can help children to develop their play.

CULTURAL INFLUENCES

It is important to remember that play is influenced by cultural setting and atmosphere. This book is rooted in the cultural context of the UK. Currently, in England and other countries of the UK there is great interest in the education and care of babies and toddlers. Although, as yet, there is no curriculum framework for this age group (0–3), adults are fascinated by the way children learn and they want to help even the youngest children to learn well.

❛ A quiet revolution has been taking place in the education of children in the early years ❜, according to the Parliamentary All-Party Report of the Education Sub-committee on Early Years (December, 2000).

CURRICULUM GUIDANCE

From September 2000, the new Foundation Stage was introduced in England, for children from three years of age to the end of the reception year. The key reference document for this stage in the child's education is *Curriculum Guidance for the Foundation Stage* (QCA, 2000). This takes priority over any other guidance (for example, the National Literacy or Numeracy strategies). Ofsted inspectors will use the book *Inspecting Schools 3–11* to inform their reports. Page 19 states that it is not required for any setting to follow the literacy hour or daily maths lesson in the reception year.

The *Curriculum Guidance for the Foundation Stage* document is also one on which Ofsted Inspections of different early children settings are based. By following the key reference document, practitioners will quite naturally, and with no extra work, be making the links necessary to cover all the elements of the National Strategies for Numeracy and Literacy in the reception year. This will give confidence to reception class teachers, who, until the introduction of the Foundation Stage in England, were pulled in contradictory directions, confused and demoralised. This official document has the same legal status as other National Curriculum stage documents. It is evidence based, and it supports the importance of learning through play in the early childhood curriculum.

In paragraph 49 of the Select Committee's report, it confirms that the Foundation Stage document gives a new approach to reception teachers, who now have the autonomy **not** to introduce the literacy hour or daily mathematics lesson. 'This approach responds to the concerns raised in evidence that much reception class provision was too formal.' (Select Committee Report, paragraph 49, p.xv.)

The Curriculum Guidance for the Foundation Stage states (QCA, 2000) that: ❛ *Well-planned play is a key way in which children learn with enjoyment and challenge during the Foundation Stage.* ❜

This statement links with the emphasis on learning through play in the Welsh, Northern Ireland and Scottish national early childhood curriculum documents for a similar age group.

It is important to remember that human children have the biological possibility to play. It would, therefore, be very unfortunate if this book was about helping only children in England to learn through their play.

Although the book will help practitioners in England to work with children in the given framework, it does not isolate English practitioners from the rest of the world and the way that it works with children.

We shall, therefore, look at how we can help all children to learn through their play using three strands:

1. the traditional early childhood curriculum approach of the pioneers

2. developing the tradition into a modern approach using the evidence from research and theory

3. the requirements of government for the early childhood curriculum (using the English core reference document, QCA, 2000).

The English document *Curriculum Guidance for the Foundation Stage* (QCA, 2000) helps practitioners to assess children's development (by observing and interpreting how a particular child is learning).

It also encourages adults to develop individual stepping stones (QCA, 2000) for children, unknowingly, to make their personal journeys towards the early learning goals. Most children (but by no means all) will reach these by the end of the Foundation Stage. Children in Scotland and Northern Ireland, unlike children in Wales and England, are not required to reach goals. Instead they are offered opportunities to learn particular things.

It is important to remember that most early childhood experts in England are unhappy about the early learning goals, and would prefer documents more like those in Scotland and Northern Ireland, which give children opportunities to experience particular areas of learning.

Key

The evidence which underpins the Foundation Stage core reference document strongly suggests that it is not good for young children to be subjected to early formal teaching.

The evidence comes from:

■ longitudinal studies (NFER, Sharp and Hutchison, 1997)

■ cross-cultural studies (Bruce, 2000)

■ psychology and brain studies (POST, 2000, Carter, 1999)

This means that it is important for those spending time with children in the foundation years to understand the importance of well-planned play (QCA, 2000) as a key to learning, in ways which both support and extend children.

This book is designed to help adults create stepping stones for children that will lead them into well-planned play. Those spending time with children can see how play begins in babyhood and toddler times, and how to build on basic play. They can then help children to develop more complex free-flowing play (Bruce, 1991) in the Foundation Years.

It is to be hoped that colleagues reading this book and working outside the English context will bear with the references to the *English Curriculum Guidance for the Foundation Stage* document sprinkled throughout the book. It cannot be stressed too strongly that, if adults playing with children at home or in early childhood group settings use the time-honoured principles of the pioneers, updated through current research and theory, the legal requirements of the English document will be more than fulfilled. This can be demonstrated through a good record-keeping system.

This book, although it emphasises the importance of play in relation to the English Foundation Stage document, will not be so culturally narrow that it has no meaning beyond England.

Summary

At the end of the book (page 125), you will find a summary of the main points made in the book. It gives the important points about play, not just in England, but across time and space.

1

Setting the scene for learning through play (0–6)

Play in babyhood

Babies need to spend time with people who encourage their play. In everyday life babies inevitably come into contact with people. They need to be changed, fed, washed, and clothed. They go with people to the shops, and to meet older brothers and sisters from school. They are cuddled and bounced on people's knees. These are all wonderful opportunities for play.

Sometimes play will be with objects, and sometimes with people.

Babies play using their sense of touch, sight, smell, hearing, taste and using feedback from their movements. As their physical co-ordination develops, helped along by the play they engage in, they begin to be able to hold objects, look at things, reach for things, and put them in their mouths.

When they learn to let go and release an object, a whole new kind of play opens up. Peekaboo play is a huge step forward. The play is enjoyable, but it is also intellectually and emotionally challenging. Trying to work out where something has gone is a puzzle. But having an object vanish, just as you thought you were going to hold it, is a bit frustrating. Adults need to be sensitive in play, so that frustration does not take over from enjoyment. When play fades away, so does learning of the deepest kind.

In Chapter 3, we shall observe a new baby in her early days of play. Most books on babies write theoretically about it. In this book, by using the narrative observation approach (which gathers a description of the play and later analyses it), play comes alive as we see it free flowing along through real babies, and in children at home and in early childhood settings.

Play during the toddler years

Toddler time is a crucial period for the development of play. It is the time when play has the possibility to develop the features which use rehearsal of roles, pretending, imagining and creating play props.

This is all part of the symbolic explosion, which occurs as the toddler turns into a talker and a player with symbols. You may like to look at the definitions box on page 4 which explains these terms.)

Toddlers have strong images of the past and future that allow them to imagine.

They are very social and, as they work out their identity (Who am I? Who is me?), they begin to realise that other people are different from them (Who are you?). They can imitate what others do. They take on the role of being someone else, usually by imitating their actions. They do not yet empathise with the role. For example, they will say, 'I ironing for the baby'. They imitate the actions of an adult ironing. But, as yet, they are not deeply in the role of being the character doing the ironing. That will develop later.

Toddlers are beginning to use the symbols of their culture. The iron is a symbol in this play scenario. The toy iron stands for a real one. It allows the toddler to rehearse, quite safely, roles that adults take on.

Play in the foundation years

Children from three to six years of age (and beyond) need:

- people who help them to play
- places to play
- materials for play props.

The English *Curriculum Guidance for the Foundation Stage* core reference document (QCA, 2000) says that the role of the adult is crucial in helping children to develop their play. In other cultural contexts, in other parts of the world, play is usually handed on from generation to generation of children, without adult support (Rogoff, 1998).

In the English context, adults are helpful to children as they play, because they:

- ■ observe children at play (as we will see in Chapter 3), in order to be informed about children's learning

- ■ use their observations to support and extend the play by planning and resourcing a challenging environment (e.g. setting up a shop, or going to the park, as in Chapters 4 and 6)

- ■ create appropriate stepping stones with particular children in mind, helping children to learn through their play and develop towards the early learning goals

- ■ engage in the play, and encourage the development of communication (both non-verbal and spoken) through play

- ■ know when to take a back seat, and let children develop the play without invasion or adult domination.

In this book, we shall see examples of children at home and in group settings where they are helped to learn through well-planned play. There is nothing like observing real children for gaining an insight into working with them. The book will, therefore, help parents, childminders and practitioners in group settings to develop play through observation.

LEARNING THROUGH PLAY

The Curriculum Guidance for the Foundation State (QCA, 2000) says that teaching ❝ means systematically helping children to learn so that they are helped to make connections in their learning and are actively led forward, as well as helped to reflect on what they have already learnt ❞.

Play helps children to make connections in their learning. In Chapter 3 we shall look at the 12 features of free-flow play as a tool for analysing the play. Feature 12 emphasises that play orchestrates learning. It helps children to bring together what they know in a connected and whole way.

Play helps children to be led forward actively in their learning. Extending learning means leading children forward.

However, helping children to play requires the most sophisticated teaching strategies of all. Although the adult leads the child forward, the child must also have the opportunity to reflect on what they have already learnt. Children who are encouraged to do this are easier to lead forward. They are easier to teach, because, through their play, they have been able to understand and bring meaning to their learning. This means they keep coming back for more!

In each chapter of Part 2, we explore a different way to emphasise the powerful and long-lasting learning which becomes possible when, in their play, children are taught to reflect on what they have learnt.

The box below contains definitions which cover some of the phrases you will come across as you read this book.

Definitions

The concept of play
This is a way of thinking about play which is shared by experts and agreed between them.

Creativity
The imagination makes images in the mind. Creativity is the process by which children turn these images into creations. They try out ideas, feelings and relationships in their role play or pretend play, make props for their play or find things to be used as play props. They might paint, make music, dance, make constructions in block play, or make models with found materials or clay.

In the context of play, creativity is more of a *process* than a product. The richer the creative process (the trying out of the imagination), the richer the product (the play scenario, the construction, the song, the dance etc.)

Free-flow play
Free-flow play arises out of 12 features of play which have been identified as important in its development. When the 12 features are considered together, it is possible to assess whether or not the play is of sufficient quality to be called free-flow play (Bruce, 1991, 1996). The 12 features are covered in more detail on page 30 and are referred to throughout.

Imagination
This is the rearrangement of past experiences in new and fascinating ways (McKellar, 1957). The imagination makes images in the mind about ideas, thoughts, feelings and relationships with the self, others and the universe.

Becoming a symbol-user
The process of becoming a symbol-user involves young children, from toddler times onwards, in making one thing stand for another. For example, during play in the garden, a twig might stand for a knife. A leaf might stand for a plate. A mud pie might stand for the cake, which is to be cut. The twig, leaf and mud pie are not really a knife, plate or cake. They are symbols that stand for those things. The child *is not* the grandmother about to cut the cake on her ninetieth birthday. She is *pretending* to be the grandmother. She is using symbolic behaviour. The child is a symbol-user.

Summary

This chapter has brought together several views of play.

- The traditional view, arising out of the work of late nineteenth- and early twentieth-century pioneers of the early childhood curriculum in the UK, that play is of central importance in helping children to learn.

- Evidence of a modern kind, that play supports and extends children in their learning, especially when it is well planned.

- the QCA view (2000) set out in the *Curriculum Guidance for the Foundation Stage* in the English cultural context only.

Bringing together these three strands shows that, whichever way play is approached, it is important in early childhood.

For children in the English Foundation Stage, if the first two strands are followed (i.e. using the traditional heritage of the pioneers, and using evidence from theory and research) then play will be well planned and children will learn in deep, broad and lasting ways. The third strand will be addressed naturally as a result.

2 Fair play in early childhood practice

·············

Studying play

Most people in the world pay no intellectual attention at all to childhood play. They do not consciously develop it in their children. Families and carers do not spend huge amounts of their time studying the detail of a child's progress in learning to sit, crawl, walk or talk. These things just happen naturally. It is the same with childhood play – it is usually just thought of as a part of growing up. It is not usual for it to be discussed or studied.

It is only a minority of people who have made childhood play a subject of study. However, those who do study young children at play, and who perhaps even join in with their play, often begin by looking at children in middle childhood (8–13 years). They usually find themselves becoming more and more fascinated with how play begins to develop and burgeon in early childhood (under 8 years).

The serious study of childhood play began with the pioneers of the early childhood curriculum. Since then, a world movement has developed and led to an International Charter of Human Rights. This has in it Article 44 which states the child's Right to Play .This is not about giving children time off work, which would be *recreation*. As we shall see in this book, the right to play is about helping children to learn in the deepest ways possible for their early years of life.

Western early childhood education and care

THE PIONEERS

Friedrich Froebel (1782–1852) put the study of childhood play

6

on the Western European map. He took the natural play of children and gave it status. It is of central importance in his philosophy for the education and care of young children. Over the years, he increasingly developed a curriculum around the child's free play, which he came to believe was the highest form of learning.

Froebel's ideas spread across Europe and reached the USA, where kindergartens were also established on a wide scale. In the UK his philosophy of education influenced pioneers such as Margaret McMillan (1860–1931) and Susan Isaacs (1885–1948).

The British nursery schools developed by Margaret McMillan were emulated throughout the world, and still are. In England, they are at the heart of the Government's Early Excellence Programme.

Susan Isaacs established the Child Development Department at the University of London in the 1930s. She trained students to observe, describe, analyse, study and develop childhood play. She understood that grounded theory underpins both practice and further theory. This is because gathering data through careful observation informs researchers, who can then build theories of their own.

MODERN WESTERN EXPERTS

Cross-cultural issues

The study of play by experts such as Susan Isaacs began in the first half of the twentieth century. It grew from the understanding of child development that emerged from Western Europe and the USA. The study of play has been heavily influenced by the discipline of psychology.

Experts researching play in the Western world have been criticised. Gunilla Dahlberg et al (1999) argue that it may not be appropriate to suggest that Western ways of looking at play can be applied cross culturally. It may be that Western experts are locked into their culture, and cannot see beyond.

Fleer (1995), who has studied Australian aboriginal children, challenges Western experts to consider whether it is appropriate to encourage play in all children. She suggests that the children she studied did not play, and that it is not necessary for them to do so. She argues that we cannot assume that play is an essential part of childhood for every child in the world.

Key

This book takes the approach that play comes in many forms. It is very complex, and difficult to describe or study. So, there will be huge cultural variations.

Perhaps, the children Fleer studied may play differently to children in Western Europe or the USA. Although play is an important means by which children begin to use the symbols of their culture, it is not the only way. The brain has evolved so that children can reach the same kinds of learning (in this case knowing how to use symbols) in a variety of ways.

Similarly, not all children crawl in the same way before they walk (Rowland, 2000). The vast majority crawl on their hands and knees. Some bottom shuffle along. Some do roly polies. Obviously, the most used method of getting about is very effective, but less conventional approaches to moving around are also possible.

Most children in the world play, and this helps them:

■ to become symbol-users (see page 4)

■ to think in abstract ways that take them beyond the here and now

■ to develop theory of mind (an understanding of the way others think and feel, and relate to people, see Chapter 7)

■ to make changes, transforming their lives and events using the imagination and creating alternative, possible worlds

■ to be flexible thinkers, so that intelligence continues to develop throughout life.

Play is a highly effective way to do these things. Children have a biological predisposition to play. However, in some cultural contexts some children, like the unconventional crawlers, will develop as symbol-users and learn to appreciate the ideas and feelings of other people in different ways. Just as it would be wrong to insist that all children should crawl in the same way, so it would be wrong to suggest that, because a minority of children do not use play as a central way of learning, it is not useful for any children to be encouraged into it.

Key

We need to respect human and cultural differences, but we also need to value the commonalities between human children (Bruce, 1997).

The concept of 'play' changes over time, even within one cultural context

Helen May (1999) argues that the way childhood play is viewed is not just subject to cultural variation. It also varies across historic time. The Western way of looking at the concept of play has been different during each decade. Each generation reinterprets the way it regards childhood play.

The human brain has the potential to play

The human brain is able, from the start of life, to take in experiences of people and objects, places and events. We know that:

■ babies need people and real physical experiences in order to develop

■ babies are able to use their innate knowledge (the knowledge they are born with) as a means of learning more

■ according to Colwyn Trevarthen (1998), babies arrive already equipped to be interested in faces and voices, and with an innate sense of a world with people in it.

BABIES ARE BORN TO BE SYMBOL-USERS

According to researchers such as Gopnik, Meltzoff and Kuhl (1999), babies are self-programmed to learn more than they know when they are born. They learn through experience.

We don't have to motivate babies to become symbol-users. To be a symbol-user means being able to make one thing stand for something else – the doll stands for the baby. Symbols have the power to help humans of all ages think beyond the here and now. The child might pretend the doll is the baby, alongside a real baby being bathed. However, we often see children pretend a doll is the baby when the real baby is no longer there. They show in their play how they watched the baby being bathed yesterday (past), or that they will help to bath the baby later (future).

Humans arrive as new-borns already equipped to develop this ability. The world they experience with people and objects 'triggers' the process to begin developing, so that between two and five years there is typically a symbolic explosion, which shows up in the child's play. The beginning of the ability to play using symbols forms an important part of this symbolic explosion, according to the findings of Western research.

The link between symbols and imagination

Being a symbol-user also helps children to become imaginative and creative. Images form in the mind from an early age. Even very young babies remember faces. They have an image of people they love and know well, which means they can recognise family and friends. By about seven months they may even show 'stranger fear' of someone who looks different from the image they have formed of what a human face should look like.

Imagination is about taking images, and rearranging them in the mind in new and fascinating ways. Imagination occurs when children go beyond the here and now into the past (recognising) and into the future (rearranging the past into something new and different) (McKeller, 1957).

The ability to adapt in a changing world requires flexibility, openness and an ability to respond creatively to new ideas, feelings, relationships, situations and physical circumstances. These qualities demonstrate intelligence. Human beings are probably the most adaptive animals and play helps children to be flexible thinkers.

Key

To summarise, children play because it helps them to:

- *become symbol-users*
- *develop abstract thought*
- *understand other people's ideas, feelings and relationships*
- *imagine alternative worlds and ways of doing things*
- *create these in play scenarios*
- *stay flexible and so develop their intelligence.*

You may like to look back at page 4 for an explanation of some terms.

Why do humans have a long childhood?

FLEXIBLE THINKING AND INTELLIGENCE

A lengthy childhood keeps thinking flexible, and helps intelligence to grow.

Human beings have a long childhood so that they stay flexible and delay acting in narrow ways. Other animals do not have the possibility to delay inflexible thinking or feelings, and so do not, through having a long childhood, develop richly in their ability to use symbols. Neither do they continue to grow in intelligence. They are, quite literally, stuck in their ways for the whole of their adult lives.

A blackbird can only sing a limited set of tunes. Its alarm call does not vary. The blackbird's mating dance follows a set formula. These behaviours are inflexible. This means a blackbird does not need a long childhood in which to learn these things. These patterns of symbolic behaviour are innate. However, they are triggered into action through experience with other birds. The variations of the song of blackbirds living in different parts of the UK are very slight.

The impact of living with other people, and experience of life, causes physical changes in the brain of a human child across the years of childhood and even into adulthood. So, the human brain keeps changing because of the people we meet, and the experiences we have with them. Human babies have the potential to begin to use a wide range of symbols and symbolic behaviour by the time they are toddlers. During toddler times, human children typically explode into using language (spoken and signed), dance, arts, music, drama, literature, science, and mathematical and logical forms of symbolic behaviour. During this period, their free-flow play has the potential to develop rapidly.

The development of language and play

HOW BABIES AND TODDLERS BECOME 'CITIZENS OF THE WORLD'

Free-flow play (Bruce, 1991) opens up rich opportunities for symbolic behaviour during the toddler period. According to Gopnik, Meltzoff and Kuhl (1999) the development of spoken or signed language is becoming established or being 'hardwired' into the brain as a universal and cross-cultural symbolic behaviour. But is symbolic, free-flow play also a cross-cultural behaviour?

It is more difficult to study free-flow play than language development, but it too is likely to be hardwired into the brain.

To compound the problem, there are huge variations in the way that this process is triggered into action. However, just because something is difficult to study doesn't make it less important.

Gopnik, Meltzoff and Kuhl (1999) suggest that all human children (unless there is a disability, or delay in development), no matter where they are in the world, are born with the potential in their brains to:

- study and remember faces
- turn facial expressions into feelings
- learn how objects move
- work out how objects disappear
- link cause and effect
- work out how to categorise objects
- work out how the sounds of language divide
- link information from the different senses by forming images
- transform two-dimensional pictures into three-dimensional objects.

These researchers, however, do not focus on whether play is something all human children have the possibility of developing (providing this is triggered by their experiences with other people, and objects).

But they do explore the way babies learn spoken or signed languages. There may well be some resonances here which help us to link what is known about language development with what is also likely to happen in the development of free-flow play.

They suggest (Gopnik et al, 1999) that babies are 'citizens of the world'. This means that babies all over the world are capable of becoming speakers and listeners. Language use is one kind of symbol use. However, they point out that, as babies grow up in their particular culture, with a particular group of people, the babies also become 'culture-bound specialists' (Gopnik et al, 1999). The way play is encouraged or constrained in a particular family or culture will influence the development of the child.

Babies can only learn the spoken languages they hear. They can only play in the ways people show them. Experience influences the forms that language or play will take. Hearing babies usually learn to speak a spoken language, unless, for example, they are growing up in a community of profoundly deaf people where sign language is the norm. In this case, they will learn to sign, using gesture and finger movements, and facial expression. Babies in the USA tend to play with adults (Rogoff, 1998), whereas babies in Borneo learn about play through other children.

During childhood the brain can easily develop spoken or signed language, or both. After a decade, the window of opportunity for the development of language (spoken or signed) begins to shut. It doesn't slam. It gradually closes (Blakemore, 2001).

The fact is that some children, by the age of six, can speak and understand several languages and, although it is unusual, can also use sign language fluently. Such children are said to be multi-lingual.

To be multi-lingual is to be a proficient and flexible symbol-user. It means the child, who has developed a mother tongue and is fluent in other languages, is already rich in symbolic behaviour. Play helps children to try out the spoken or signed languages they learn.

LANGUAGE, PLAY AND CULTURE ARE CLOSELY LINKED

Children participate in their cultures, because to speak a language fluently involves learning the cultural aspects in which the language is rooted. For example, Gujurati speakers do not use 'thank you' in the way of English speakers. In Gujurati, this word is used to express deep and sincere gratitude. In English it is used as an everyday word, for example, to thank the bus conductor who gives the ticket in exchange for money. This cultural distinction will show in the child's play and language.

Children who have experienced different cultural conventions are already able to understand how to manipulate different symbols to mean different things, sometimes with sophisticated layers of meaning. Because they know intimately about differing cultural conventions and symbols, they are not destined to be narrow 'culture-bound specialists'.

Play helps children to experiment with language in ways which are not narrowly culture bound. It encourages children to be citizens of the world, because it helps them to create a variety of ways of talking and doing things, which they experiment with in their play scenarios.

'CULTURE-BOUND SPECIALISTS'

Children who are monolingual are able to function at high levels symbolically, but only within their own language. Neither do they have the advantage of participating deeply in the different ways that different languages work. Consequently, their lives are inevitably narrower in perspective.

For example, an English-speaking parent might give a drink to a baby saying, 'Here's your cup'. The emphasis would be on the word 'cup'. A Korean parent is likely to say, 'It's moving in', stressing the movement of the cup.

To speak both languages means the toddler learns the words to express ideas and feelings about the cup *and* how it moves, in several different ways. A monolingual child will only learn to talk about the cup, or the movement in one way. The fascinating thing is that all babies, as they turn to toddlers, seem to learn to use words for cups and movements, whatever the language and cultural variations. It is just that some children have more choice, and flexibility.

Developing a system of meaning through play

The important thing seems to be that toddlers, throughout the world, develop a system of meaning which helps them into both language and play. Jean Mandler (1966) suggests they do this in three ways.

---

1. Through daily living, babies are helped to look at objects by people. They gradually form images of the objects around them, by relating to the people.

2. Babies are also given objects, like cups, to manipulate, and they try to work out the difference between the three-dimensional and the two-dimensional world. This has great variation across cultures.

3. Babies usually crawl, and go to fetch objects they want, or they move to join people.

For most babies, it is not necessary to teach them how to look at objects and people, or to manipulate and play with objects. They do this on their own in their play. Through their play, for example, they confirm which objects move on their own. They establish the difference between animals and objects, still objects, dead or sleeping animals and people. They explore mechanical things. Again there is enormous cultural variation in this. Toddlers and young children are curious about how to make an object or person move, fall, or bounce. They try to put one object inside another. These early experiences exploring the sense, space, movement, images, objects and people open up possibilities for play.

Again, children in different cultural situations will develop different systems of meaning which, as Jean Mandler suggests, lead them into play and other kinds of symbolic behaviour in deeply different ways. The way that Australian Aboriginal children do this will have little in common with the ways that English children do it in their play.

Key

There is an important message here. Malaguzzi (1996), the Italian educator who pioneered the development of the early childhood curriculum in Reggio Emilia, talked about the Hundred Languages of Children; meaning that there are many ways to play.

Play looks different in different cultural contexts

Different cultures and communities encourage children to play in different ways.

- Adults may or may not join in the play.
- Children may or may not be given toys to play with.
- Children may play in mixed age groups away from adults.
- They may be expected to grow out of play by five years, or in middle childhood (by nine years or so).
- Rich childhood play may be linked with adult creativity and imagination.

CULTURAL CONTEXTS IN THIS BOOK

Children growing up in the UK today are growing up in a multi-cultural world. They often speak more than one language. The children that we follow in Part 2 of this book live in an urban context in one of the biggest cities in the world. We shall see how they are learning to play and become symbol-users in rich and varied ways.

These children have some things in common:

■ They are all human.

■ They all live in an urban context.

■ They will all learn to speak English.

■ They will all attend some kind of early childhood education or care group provision.

■ In the group they attend, adults will encourage them to play.

There will be major differences in the lives of these children.

■ Some will speak English as an additional language.

■ Some will be only children and play alone at home.

■ Some will play with adults at home, and some will not.

If there are such variations within a group of children growing up in the same city, it doesn't take much to imagine how there will be far reaching differences in the play of children growing up in different parts of the world.

Principles of equality and inclusion in play

DISABILITY

For some children, play is a challenge. Play, even of a basic kind, may be slow to develop, or the play may remain in an emergent form. Very often, sensitive awareness by people and the careful introduction of objects, music and movement can open up the play, even when such development seemed unlikely. It is of central importance that adults working with children with multi-disabilities and complex needs rise to such challenges.

An inclusive approach to play means that there must be a great emphasis on creating an environment which encourages play, and which provides access to play for children who need special help. The English QCA (2000) document stresses this throughout. Robert Orr (2000) stresses the need to consider access for children who are wheelchair-users.

The Danish educator, Lilli Nielsen (1992) believes that all children should have the right to be in a 'den', which is something most children enjoy making for themselves, under tables, or under trees or bushes. She has developed this possibility through the 'Little Room' for children who have multi-disabilities. The adult makes a house around the child, based on their observations of what the child enjoys.

❝ The child experiences his (her) world by means of all sensory modalities: he/she experiments with the world, explores it and creates worlds that are his/her own. Through all this he/she achieves the perception of being a part of the surrounding world, and as being separated from objects and persons in this world – as a self. ❞
(Nielsen, 1992)

GENDER

Children who move beyond basic play into free-flow play develop the possibility to broaden their view of people. We saw in the Introduction how free-flow play facilitates understanding of the way people from different families and cultures think. It is the features relating to role play, rehearsal for adult life, and pretend which contribute to this.

Adults have a tendency to accept the world as it is. They say this is being realistic. The problem is, that in doing this, they constrain children's play. Free-flowing play has the possibility to broaden a child's view of other people. Play is partly about helping children to live in a real world, but it is also about how things might be, for better or worse. Adults who 'shift their pedagogic gaze' (MacNaughton, 2000) can help children consider life from the point of view of different genders, and to be aware of and respect differences. For example, boys can be pregnant and give birth during play (BBC Radio 4, Tuning into Children, 1999).

Boys often need support in order to move into role play. Action research by Penny Holland (1999), in her work setting, suggests that the three- and four-year-old boys needed help from an adult to move from posturing with weapons and hero costumes into play scenarios with fuller characterisations and stories that broadened their play. Her research cannot be generalised, but it raises interesting questions to explore.

What do children play at?

- Children at play can create new worlds.
- They experiment with worlds that are better than those that exist in their experience.
- They experiment with worlds full of evil.

- They develop strategies to create good and evil.

They make stories and characters in their play scenarios which lead into complex areas of later study and interest.

- Adult literature – drama, poetry and prose.
- Study of people, past, present and future – evolution, archaeology, history, political theory, geography.

They make places into new and alternative worlds.

- They create work environments – shops, factories, markets, farms, hospitals.
- They make beautiful places – seashore scenes, fairylands, palaces.
- They make adventures – in deserts, under the sea, in outer space, on holiday.
- They make dangerous and safe places – with goodies, baddies, families, friends, monsters, superheroes and heroines.

MAKING PLAY FAIR

Fair play in early childhood practice means that we need to encourage children to:

- become more creative and flexible than they would otherwise be
- be more spiritually aware (knowing and relating to the self, others, and the universe)
- be able to experience fully through the arts (such as drama, paintings, sculpture, dance, music, etc.) both humorous and cathartic moments that make life more bearable and manageable.

Summary

Fair play for children does not mean that all children have to play in the same way, wherever they live in the world. What is right for one family, culture or society may not be right for another. The promotion of fair play for children means that we need to celebrate differences and commonalities in childhood play in an inclusive way. We need to provide access to play for children with special educational needs and disabilities, for boys and girls.

3

Observing and describing play (babies)

• • • • • • • • • •

Theory and practice should feed each other

We can make all the theories in the world about play, but a theory is no use at all if it doesn't help us in practice. We need working theories.

WHY DO WE NEED THEORIES?

Theories help us to predict and anticipate how children might behave and react. They help us to structure what we observe. Theories help us to make sense of what we see.

However, we need to be careful not to use theories which narrow down our thinking about childhood play. We want theories which open up our thinking, and which challenge what we thought we knew. This will help us to develop our understanding of childhood play.

Key

Theories help us to:

- *observe children (and/or adults) at play*
- *describe children (and/or adults) at play*
- *analyse and make sense of what we see.*

When we analyse play, we find ourselves linking what we have found with what other people (theorists) have found. We may find our observations fit with theories. We may find they do not. This will help us to think deeply about play, and to keep exploring and finding out more about childhood play.

The famous Nobel prize-winning scientist, Richard Feynman, said that, ❛ The thing that doesn't fit is the most interesting. ❜

Observing babies

OBSERVING THE BABY'S PLAY USING NARRATIVE OBSERVATION TECHNIQUES

There are many different observation techniques – different techniques are useful for different situations and purposes. It is important to find ways of observing which are appropriate to studying play. Some techniques are too simplistic for looking at a complex area such as childhood play.

Traditional narrative observation is recommended for observing and describing children and/or adults at play. It allows rich opportunities for analysing the play afterwards. This is a time-honoured approach, which has stood the test of time. It is as useful now as it was when it was first developed by Susan Isaacs in the 1930s.

THE FOUR STEPS OF NARRATIVE OBSERVATION

Narrative observation involves four steps.

1. The observer writes briefly about the context of the observation.

2. The observer writes down as exact a description as possible of what the child says and does. If other children are also involved, the observer writes down enough description of the conversations and actions of other children to give a clear picture of the target child.

3. The observation can then be analysed and interpreted.

4. The observation can be linked with the observations made by other people of this child. It can also be linked with theories to see if it fits or challenges research findings.

This approach to observation is useful for the following reasons.

■ It discourages the observer from making value-laden judgements about families and children.

■ It challenges the observer to reflect on cultural differences and to respect families and children, and to take an inclusive approach to special educational needs and disability.

- The observer does not spoil the observation by analysing throughout, because the analysis comes as a later step, after gathering the on-the-spot description.

- The description gives enough detail for the observer to be able to analyse later, without making wild claims that are unsupported by evidence.

- The observation can be given a particular focus for analysis. In this book, the focus when analysing observations will be on childhood play.

- The analysis deepens when the observer makes use of current theory and research to support and illuminate the interpretation made.

It is important when observing only to describe what the child is doing or saying. An adult who starts interpreting whilst observing will spoil the observation, perhaps becoming distracted or, more seriously, seeing only those features of play which fit a particular theory.

The form on page 22 shows the different elements of a narrative observation. Some people like to write their observations on a form like this. Others prefer to note the headings, but to write about them on a plain piece of paper, which doesn't look like a form.

Photographs are very useful in enhancing narrative observations. They can highlight some of the important moments.

Video is an invaluable modern tool for narrative observation (Haggerty, 1997). If Susan Isaacs had been alive today, she would surely have made use of video as a rich description of exactly what happened. The advantage is that the video tape can be replayed again and again. Each time it is viewed, fascinating new observations are made, and the analysis can be deepened. Video analysis seems to open up the possibility of adding layer upon layer of meaning and insight to the observation. However, it must be used with care and sensitivity as it can make some children feel self-conscious if they are not familiar with it. Once it becomes established though, children take little notice of it (Athey, 1990).

The narrative observation gives an exact description of what has happened, and the communication that has taken place. This might take the form of eye contact between a baby or child and adults. You might note the tone of voice used, or some other form of non-verbal communication with the baby or child. Non-verbal communication is important throughout life, and spoken language emerges out of it.

This form can be used when observing babies or children.

NARRATIVE OBSERVATION

Child's name _____

Date of observation _____

Time observation begins _____

Time observation ends _____

Short description of context in which the observation is being made

_____
_____
_____
_____

Description of what is happening

_____
_____
_____
_____

Communication (both non-verbal and spoken)

With self

_____
_____

With others

_____
_____

Adopted from Bartholomew and Bruce (1994)

Working through an observation

WHAT IS THE CULTURAL AND COMMUNITY CONTEXT?

Look at the baby in the photograph. She is only a few weeks old. Before we start observing this baby, we need to find out what is important to her family in relation to her play. We also need to find out about the baby's family. Her mother grew up in Vietnam, and came to Britain when she was 11 years of age. The mother's family also live in London, and visit regularly. She does not go out to work since having the baby.

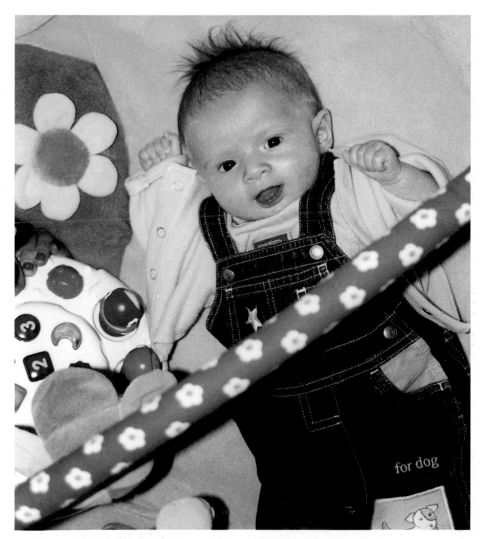

▲ Typically, babies growing up in the UK are given toys which encourage them to play.

▲ Mother shows the baby pictures painted on the wall.

The baby's father is English, and grew up in a rural area. His family visit, but live some way away in Wiltshire. Every evening, when he comes home from work, father holds and plays with the baby.

Father's younger sister (aged 13 years) has painted the wall of the baby's bedroom. Her mother explains that she is missing the extended family network, a cultural aspect of Vietnam. We have now collected quite a lot of detail about the baby's cultural and community context.

▲ Father notices the baby is gazing at something, and holds her so that she can look without being constrained. On following the line of her gaze, it seems that she is looking at the light hanging from the ceiling, which is switched on.

DESCRIBING THE PHYSICAL CONTEXT

The baby is in a room in the evening. The house lights are on, and the daylight outside is fading. Father has just arrived home from work, and wants to play with his daughter. The parents enjoy choosing what to do with her. They decide to place her on

▲ This photograph shows the physical context of the observation. A description is given on pages 25–26.

the floor on a soft cover, with toys hanging from above on a specially designed frame. The parents choose to show her a round toy with buttons on it. (This is in the photograph above.) The specially designed frame and the round toy are gifts given by the family, to celebrate the baby's birth.

We now have a description of the baby's cultural and community context, and her physical context.

Gathering observations through description

DESCRIPTION OF WHAT IS HAPPENING

The baby is placed on the mat. She has her hands clenched, and pulls her left hand towards her mouth. She looks at her father, giving eye contact. Her legs kick about, alternating as if she is gently bicycling in the air.

▲ Punching, kicking and watching.

COMMUNICATION (BOTH NON-VERBAL AND SPOKEN)

Her father talks to her as he lowers her onto the mat, saying, 'There we are'. He speaks in a higher tone than he does when talking to the mother about whether this is a good idea.

Mother joins father, and they both kneel on the floor next to the baby. She also speaks to the baby in a high voice, but speaks to the father in a normal speaking voice. She says, 'It's coming over' as she moves the round toy towards the baby.

Interpreting and analysing observations

BE AWARE OF YOUR OWN THEORIES

Everyone has personal theories which guide them through their lives. However, not many people are aware of having them. Some people believe that they are objective thinkers, but this is not humanly possible.

It would be a very boring and machine-like world if people didn't have personal theories about life. The important thing is to be *aware* that we have them, even though we don't necessarily know what they are! This is particularly important when studying play.

We noted in Chapters 1 and 2 that play varies in different parts of the world, in different cultures, and in different families. It is a certainty that each one of us will have a personal theory about childhood play. This will be influenced by our upbringing, our cultural context, and where we live in the world.

So, we need to be aware that we may have a narrow mono-cultural view of play. One of the main reasons for undertaking narrative observations is to find a way of opening up our thinking to encompass a broader view of play. Then we can help children and families to get the most out of their learning in ways which are right for them.

In the photographs of the baby, we can see that she is gazing at one or other of her parents, making eye contact with them, or looking at a light or at objects.

Next we want to focus our analysis on the baby's play. So what is going on here? It might be helpful to ask the parents to tell us what happens when they play with their baby. We can also draw on traditional and modern theories to help us analyse.

▲ The parents will be able to tell you about their baby's play.

PARENTAL EXPERTISE

The parents will want to tell us what their baby enjoys, although they might not call it play. The baby's parents say that she enjoys being on the mat, and looking at the dangling toys in the specially designed frame, but not if she is tired, uncomfortable or hungry. She also enjoys trying to reach out and touch the objects.

THE APPROACH OF THE PIONEERS OF THE EARLY CHILDHOOD CURRICULUM

It is fascinating to look at the writings of some of the pioneers of early childhood education and care in the Western world, to see what they say about play (Bruce, 1991). There are some recurring themes in their views, including features of play, which seem to link with what modern researchers think is important about play.

One way to focus this observation would be to see if any of these features of play are already emerging in this young baby.

Key

The 12 features of play

1. *In their play, children use the first-hand experiences that they have in life.*
2. *Children make up rules as they play, and so keep control of their play.*
3. *Children make play props.*
4. *Children choose to play. They cannot be made to play.*
5. *Children rehearse the future in their role play.*
6. *Children pretend when they play.*
7. *Children play alone sometimes.*
8. *Children and/or adults play together, in parallel, associatively, or co-operatively in pairs or groups.*
9. *Each player has a personal play agenda, although they may not be aware of this.*
10. *Children playing will be deeply involved, and difficult to distract from their deep learning. Children at play wallow in their learning.*
11. *Children try out their most recent learning, skills and competencies when they play. They seem to celebrate what they know.*
12. *Children at play co-ordinate their ideas, feelings and make sense of relationships with their family, friends and culture. When play is co-ordinated it flows along in a sustained way. It is called free-flow play.*

Developed from Bruce (1991 and 1996).

USING THE 12 FEATURES OF PLAY IN THE ANALYSIS

- The baby is using her senses. She is touching objects, looking at them, listening, and putting her hand in her mouth to suck and taste. She looks intently at the person she has eye contact with and, as they speak, she moves rapidly, kicking her legs about and flailing her arms. At the moment, she is gaining the first-hand experiences which she will later use in her play. (This links with feature 1.)

- She already chooses when to play and when she is not in the mood for it. Her parents are learning when she will enjoy playing, and when it is not a good time. (Feature 4.)

- She plays alone already. We will look at this in more detail in the next section. (Feature 7.)

- In this observation, there are no other children for her to play with. It is evident that she does like to play with adults, especially those she knows. (Feature 8.) Babies this young can play together. In a video made by the National Children's Bureau (1997) which builds on the work of Elinor Goldschmied, two babies are seen lying on their backs and playing with each other.

▲ Touching objects.

▲ Gazing at an object.

- She has her own play agenda. She wants to gaze at people's faces, objects near enough for her to see, and she likes to touch objects that she looks at, but not for long because it is too difficult. (Feature 9.)

- She wallows in her playing, giving it her all. (Feature 10.)

- She is already showing off her latest skills in her play. She tries to touch what she sees, which is a huge effort, but she tries again and again. (Feature 11.)

- She is bringing together what she has been learning as she plays. Her play co-ordinates her learning. She is using what she knows about objects, brightness and people's faces. (Feature 12.)

It is quite amazing to see how many of the features of free-flow play are already in evidence. Eight out of the 12 seem to be present. We can conclude that this is rich play.

The features which have yet to emerge are, unsurprisingly, those which deal with the imaginative and creative aspects of play, for example, rehearsal of roles, or pretending, making and using play props, or drawing on experience to make a play scenario.

▲ Reaching out to touch an object.

Some of the first play of this kind is, all over the world, food preparation play. Two- and three-year-olds often play at making meals, and cooking and shopping.

This baby is well on the way to free-flow play in all its aspects.

USING WHAT MODERN EXPERTS SAY IN THE ANALYSIS

Penelope Leach says (1997), ʿAlthough newborn babies cannot handle toys or take part in games, even the youngest of them can certainly get bored and lonely ...ʾ

In this play, the baby is enjoying looking at objects hanging from a play frame. Penelope Leach points out that, although babies cannot tell us what they like, we know that they look for longer at things they prefer. This baby likes to gaze at the light in the ceiling, to look into the eyes of either parent, to look at the hanging objects and the circular toy.

The hanging objects and the circular toy are at a perfect focusing distance of 20–25 cms (8–10 inches) from the bridge of her nose. This is also the distance at which we naturally hold the baby in our arms to talk to her. The light is further away but, although a blur, it can be seen. It is of interest. Babies are biologically predisposed to prefer objects near to them, if given the choice. This encourages them to focus on people, to make relationships, to talk and play with others.

Penelope Leach (1997) points out that ʿIf, armed with this information, you deliberately put things close enough to your baby's eyes for him to see them clearly, he will 'choose' to pay attention to much more subtle stimuli than brightness or movement.ʾ

Babies prefer their mother's or father's voice to that of a stranger.

Penelope Leach says (1997) that ʿUnless you are on the look-out for it, you may not notice how much your baby enjoys your voice during these first weeks ... he often listens to your voice without looking at you ... when you begin to speak to him, he will start to move excitedly.ʾ

We can see that the baby does just this when her parents speak to her as she lies on the mat with them looking down at her, smiling at her, and talking to her.

The baby is holding her hands in a tight fist. If we were to put something in her palm, she would hold it tightly in a reflex grasp. Miriam Stoppard (1990) shows how, after two months or so, the baby will hold her hand open more often, and the grasp is increasingly voluntary. But the baby cannot yet release an object she is holding.

This baby does seem to enjoy trying to touch the circular toy, because she keeps trying to do it. Her mother makes encouraging noises as she does so.

It is very interesting that her mother talks to her about the movement and direction of the toy. She says, 'It's coming over.' Someone with English as their first language would be more likely to say, 'Do you want this? It's round.' Different languages emphasise different things. Research (Talmy, 1999) suggests that all children all over the world, although their parents emphasise different things (e.g. the line of movement of an object, or the object itself), by the time they themselves begin to speak, seem to know about objects and the movements they make.

It is also interesting that both the baby's parents spoke to her in motherese and fatherese. Colwyn Trevarthen (1998) calls this kind of talking to babies in a high tone, a proto-conversation. The person speaking to the baby, as well as speaking in a high voice, also speaks slowly and emphasises important words. This is, in fact, an early sort of conversation, without words. It involves a lot of moving together, almost as if the adult and baby are in a partner dance using sound. This is the beginning of language, but it is also the beginning of dance and music and poetry. This kind of play is hugely important for later learning. It is play that lays the foundations for learning later on.

Through her play, this baby is learning the crucial things which will help her to create a system of meaning that she will develop throughout her life.

- She is looking at the faces of people and forming images.
- She is encountering objects and learning how to touch them and interact with them.
- She is listening and moving to the voices of people she loves, and feeling their movement in tune with hers.

Summary

Perhaps it is a good thing we are not aware that the play we enjoy with babies is such an education for them, or we might spoil the pleasure of it. As soon as we get serious about it, we spoil the educational benefit. As we learn more and more about human development, we must be careful not to damage the learning through play that babies engage in so energetically. This seems to be a problem in some parts of the world. Parents in the UK are very vulnerable to these pressures at this time in history.

There is talk in circles of influence on the government that a curriculum framework might be developed in England for babies and toddlers. However, this would have to be approached with extreme caution.

We must remember there is now overwhelming evidence that babies need other people to *trigger* their natural learning. This does not mean that they need other people to *control* their learning, for in doing so adults will constrain it.

In this book, the emphasis is on encouraging adults to develop their observation skills, so that they can analyse and interpret play using the heritage of the early pioneers, and current research and theory. Then adults can help children to do their own learning through play.

4

How play makes sense of learning

Human beings have a long childhood

As we saw in Chapter 2, human beings have a very long childhood compared with other mammals. Not all children in the world go to school, and many will be beginning work by the age of seven or eight. Even so, compared with a chimpanzee, a childhood of seven or eight years is still a long time.

WHY DO HUMANS HAVE A LONG CHILDHOOD?

We have a comparatively long childhood for a variety of reasons.

■ It encourages flexible thinking.

■ Flexible thinking allows intelligence to grow.

■ It allows experimentation with feelings.

■ It helps children to get their feelings under control.

■ It allows children to get inside someone else's mind, whilst remaining themselves.

■ It encourages awareness, sensitivity, empathy and understanding of others, which helps good relationships to develop.

■ It encourages children to reflect, through the appropriate process of play, on moral issues such as goodness and evil, fairness and justice.

■ It gives them opportunities to learn about their culture.

■ It gives children time to play.

Children do not play unless the process is 'triggered' by people, but they are biologically predisposed to play. So, we can say there are socio-cultural and biological aspects to play development.

Children are born with a physical brain that is genetically set to develop in ways particular to being a human. But each child's brain is also a unique brain, which is different from anyone else's. Examples of the biological aspects of development are that the child, unless there is a disability or some other constraint, will learn to sit, crawl, walk, talk and play.

These biologically-driven processes need to be triggered by other people. A baby is helpless without other people. If a baby is never spoken to or played with, that baby does not develop language or play. It is more obvious if language does not develop than if the development of play is absent.

Key

Both the biological *and* socio-cultural aspects *of development are important in the development of play.*

In Chapter 3, we observed the baby learning to play with her parents. We could also see that she has the advantage of parents who draw on two cultural influences. Both the cultural and social life of the baby is rich.

She is also beginning to explore objects, space, and to play, showing off her latest socio-cultural learning and her biological development.

Observing toddlers' play

Toddlers spend a great deal of time relating to people, exploring their own cultural and physical context, and trying to make sense of their lives through their play.

In most parts of the world, adults are not aware that the child is learning so much through their play. However, cross-cultural studies (Whiting, 1992) indicate that children in nomadic, agricultural settled, or post-industrial lifestyles all, in one way or another, seem to benefit from having space and time to play.

Some toddlers learn about play with adults. This is particularly so in the Western world of Europe and the USA. Others play mainly with older siblings (brothers and sisters). Of course, play will be different in form depending on the way the child is taught to engage in it (Rogoff, 1998).

Although toddlers growing up in the UK are often given toys, they also enjoy the cross-cultural and time-honoured play indulged in by toddlers all over the world. They will clamber on and off a chair if a chair is there, but if not, they will apply the same treatment to a person!

OBSERVING A TODDLER PLAYING WITH A CHAIR

The toddler in the photograph sequence is playing with his mother, who is about to give birth to her second baby.

Although a toddler will play about, climbing on a chair with gusto, if a person is there to share the pleasure, all the better. The toddler in the photograph looks back at his mother to check her reaction. Judy Dunn (1991) calls this 'affective tuning'.

▲ Looking back at mum – affective tuning.

During the toddler period, the baby turns from a sitter, to a crawler, to a walker, and from someone who uses only non-verbal communication to one who uses both non-verbal communication and spoken words. It is also at this time that an awareness of the reactions of others begins to develop. Out of this, an understanding of other people's feelings and thoughts will gradually develop.

The play with the chair might not have lasted so long (it was about 20 minutes) if mother had not been part of it. She gives a helping hand to lever him onto the chair when he has nearly managed it. This just keeps him from slipping off and becoming frustrated.

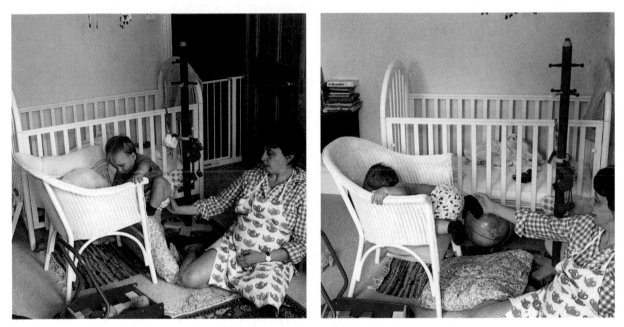

▲ A helping hand prevents frustration.

It is fascinating to see how, having done it once, he repeats getting on and off the chair over and over again. He sits in triumph and then, for a fleeting moment only, imitates the way adults sit on chairs (see page 40).

He makes contact with his mother when he stands on the chair (see page 41). It is almost as if he is saying, 'Be there for me in case I fall, but don't do anything unless I need you.'

▲ Having fun doing it again.

▲ Feeling a sense of achievement.

◀ Sitting like an adult – playing at being grown up.

Toddlers will frequently, if they feel secure enough, leave a loved person they are playing with, to fetch an object and bring it back to them. They often make a move to get to know a newcomer by offering them an object, although they usually take it back immediately!

They show people things, as if to develop a conversation through their play. They seem to 'ask' to hold objects by stretching out their arms, and holding their hands open. They might make word-like sounds as they do so (see pages 41–42).

Key

Play with people, and play with objects and space are important aspects of being a toddler growing up in the UK today.

▲ Communicating with mum.

▲ Offering an object.

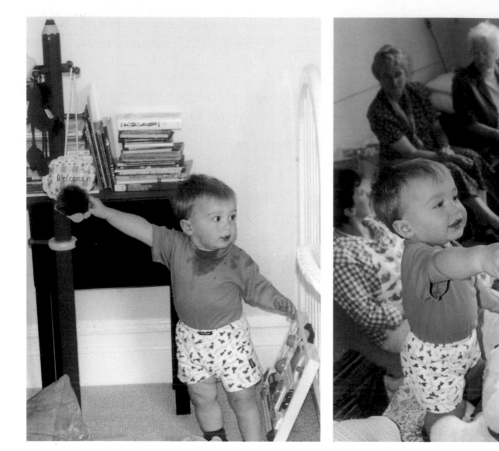

▲ Showing mum an object.　　　　▲ Reaching for an object.

Linking the observation to theory

It might be interesting to see how this toddler's play with the chair relates to the 12 features of play. In Chapter 3, we saw that the baby is already demonstrating rich play. The play develops in complexity during the toddler period, and we see that play with objects and people moves into pretend play; the child is becoming an emergent symbol-user.

It takes time, two or three years, to develop enough first-hand experience of living to be able to turn the experiences into play. This toddler is exploring experiences with people and objects in space, so that he can use what he knows in his play later on. At this time in his development, he needs to find out about chairs, and other objects. He needs to manipulate, discover and explore, using his senses and movement of his increasingly co-ordinated body.

Jean Mandler (1996) suggests it is developing a system of meaning that will lead the toddler into increasingly more complex layerings in his play. He can already form images of experiences he has had with people and objects. He spends masses of time manipulating objects, and getting to know the people with whom he lives and spends time.

He can move about freely now that he can walk. Being mobile means he can go and fetch objects, or show people things that interest him, by taking them with him, or calling them to him. Being able to walk has given him more control over his life, but it is also a little scary to be so free. He needs constant reassurance by having people he loves near him. This gives him the confidence to have independent adventures on the other side of the room, or even out of view.

USING THE 12 FEATURES OF PLAY IN THE ANALYSIS

Key

The 12 features of play

1. *Using first-hand experiences*
2. *Making up rules*
3. *Making props*
4. *Choosing to play*
5. *Rehearsing the future*
6. *Pretending*
7. *Playing alone*
8. *Playing together*
9. *Having a personal agenda*
10. *Being deeply involved*
11. *Trying out recent learning*
12. *Co-ordinating ideas, feelings and relationships for free-flow play*

(Adapted from Bruce 1991, 1996)

■ These kinds of first-hand experience will lead him to engage in pretend play, and so become a symbol-user. (Feature 1.)

- He is on the brink of making up his own rules as he plays with the chair. He has made a little sequence of climbing on, turning round and sitting, and then standing up, reaching out for his mother's hand to steady him and help him down. This is repeated over and over again. It is his own little rule, which he applies as he plays. (Feature 2.)

- He is not yet making his own play props. But he is finding and using props from his environment for his play. He uses the chair as a play prop, and also at different points, he uses the large and small teddies, the wooden toy, and the hanging pole.

  In this, he is like children all over the world. He makes use of what he can find, and turns them into play props. He has a lot more freedom to do this than the baby in Chapter 3. He can walk to fetch and carry objects he wants. He can walk over to a person he wants to be near, or away from them if he wishes. He can hold objects in his hands, but he can do more than the baby in that he can open and close his hands. This means he can choose to pick something up. He doesn't have to wait for something to be put in his hand for him to grasp. He can also drop or release an object from his grip. This allows him to play in a variety of ways with objects. (Feature 3.)

- He cannot be made to play. Anyone who tries to make a toddler do something they do not want to do will have difficulty. However, because, as Judy Dunn (1988) says, toddlers are affectively tuned, they are very interested in what other people are doing. Providing, like the baby, the toddler is not tired, uncomfortable or hungry, he is likely to be interested in what the people around him are doing.

  There is a difference between *copying* and *imitating* what others do. Copying is doing passively exactly what the other person does. Imitating means taking the idea and transforming it into your own. By imitating the toddler is able to reconstruct a situation in a way that makes meaning for him. We catch a glimpse of this in his play with the chair. He has experience of seeing people sit on chairs. He chooses to do so at one point in his play, but not for long. He is imitating this movement, and incorporating it into his play sequence. If we tried to make him sit on a chair, he would probably refuse! Children need to choose when and what to play.

  Children who, from an early age, choose their play do not remain totally dependent on adults in their play. They begin to lead their play, and to structure it for themselves. Such children are more likely to become creative thinkers as adults. (Feature 4.)

■ This little boy is not yet involved in role play with the chair. For a brief moment, he sits on the chair like an adult, but this has not yet become role play. It contains the seed of it though. (Feature 5.)

■ He doesn't pretend the chair is part of a play scenario with a story and characters. This possibility will come later. (Feature 6.)

■ He does play alone, but usually in the company of his mother or other members of the family, or within a friendship group. To be entirely alone at play, he would need to feel very secure. Toddlers soon need company. In evolutionary terms, this is probably because they would be in danger if they went off alone. Young mammals need to stay with adults until they know enough to be safe alone. (Feature 7.)

■ He can play in parallel with other children, but there aren't any present on this occasion. His mother is sensitive to his needs and supports his play alongside him. They co-operate together. He can extend his play with someone he is close to, like his mother, and this is because she is willing to let him lead the play. It will be interesting to see if he becomes a play leader when he widens his circle, and begins to play co-operatively with other children. Some children find it difficult to play unless they are the leader all the time. Others like to be followers. Ideally, children will experiment with being both leaders and followers in their play. This will help them to become good team members, but also able to lead. (Feature 8.)

■ He has a strong play agenda. He wants to play with the chair, and he wants to go up and down, and be on top of it. (Feature 9.)

■ He is very involved in his play, and cannot be distracted from it. He is wallowing in his play with the chair. (Feature 10.)

■ He is definitely triumphant about his ability to climb up onto the chair. This is a fairly recent piece of learning. It really is as if he needs to show it off. This is a fine example of the joy of learning for young children. Children who are always at the stage of struggling in their learning, and who never become competent enough to gain the mastery they need in order to enjoy what they have learnt, will become reluctant learners. For example, there are many children who never enjoy writing stories. They have not had enough experience of creating play scenarios with a story line (narrative) and characters who have adventures. Children who have not created stories in their play will find it very difficult to write stories later. Because it is very difficult for them to do, they will probably try to avoid doing it. Famous writers from

Western culture, who as children created play scenarios of a rich kind, are H.G. Wells, the Brontes (Branwell, Charlotte, Emily and Anne), and E.E. Nesbitt. They developed mastery of storytelling in their play, which later turned into creative writing.

This toddler is trying out his latest learning with skill, as he climbs and gets down from the chair. He shows technical prowess in his play. (Feature 11.)

■ He is co-ordinating what he knows about chairs, and bringing his knowledge together in his play. He sits, climbs on, links with other people, and gets down from the chair. (Feature 12.)

Play is a process

This toddler is well on the way to playing using all 12 features of play. It looks as if there is no purpose, product or outcome to what he is doing. But that is the whole point about play; it definitely should not have a purpose, product or outcome.

Play is a process. It cannot be pinned down into a product. It keeps flowing along. It keeps the learning open and flexible. The minute it has a product, it is no longer free-flowing play.

There are many kinds of very valid learning which humans engage in that do have a purpose and a product. For example, learning to cook a cake requires the cook to learn the recipe, or to be able to read it. *But this is not play*. Children at play are able to stay flexible, respond to events and changing situations, be sensitive to people, to adapt, think on their feet, and keep altering what they do in a fast-moving scene.

When the process of play is rich, it can lead children into creating rich products in their stories, paintings, dances, music making, drawings, sculptures and constructions, or in the solving of scientific and mathematical problems.

PLAY HELPS CHILDREN MAKE SENSE OF THEIR LEARNING

In short, play helps children to develop their intelligence. William Calvin (1997) says that intelligence is what you use when you don't know what to do.

Children at play don't know what is coming next. They have to work out what to do. This toddler didn't know in advance that he would feel unsteady when he stood on the chair. He had to work out what to do. He reached out for his mother's hand, which she gave him. He already knows that his mother will help him when he is in difficulty. This was an emotional response, but one in which he used his intelligence.

Key

It really does seem to be true to say that children are trying to make sense of their lives when they play.

Summary

Human children are born with the biological possibility to become flexible thinkers and to remain open to learning for the whole of their lives. Play helps intelligence to develop.

Because humans are social animals, babies and toddlers need other people to trigger the biological process of play. Babies and toddlers benefit from play with people and objects. So, the learning through play is both biological and socio-cultural.

Play helps children dare to learn, even when they are uncertain about what will happen. It creates an attitude of mind which is curious, investigative, risk taking and full of adventure.

Play is a process. It cannot be pinned down and made into a product because it needs to flow.

Play makes sense – it helps children to make sense of their lives.

5
How play helps develop abstract ideas

Moving from the present into the past and future

Play helps children to become abstract thinkers. This means that they do not have to do everything here and now. They can remember back and think forward. Their thinking can be mobile and free flowing. This is why the phrase 'free-flowing play' is so useful. It has in it the essence of what play brings to learning.

We have seen that even babies and toddlers like to play with people and objects. As they become increasingly able to co-ordinate their bodies, so their play becomes more complex. But it isn't as simple as that. It is true that they are biologically pre-programmed to develop physically, but realising what is biologically pre-programmed depends on other people, as well as on opportunities to interact with the physical world of space, objects, reasons for things and timing.

Understanding about time, space and the reasons why things happen is important for developing thinking and having ideas. Other people are essential for this kind of learning to develop. Play, talk and non-verbal communication (gesture, eye contact, different voice tones, facial expression, pauses etc.) all contribute to the development and learning of children.

Key

Spoken or signed language helps children to move beyond the here and now into the past and future.

A SENSE OF SELF

By the age of about two years, children have often become talkers or signers. Communication helps children to explore who they are.

Key

Developing a sense of 'I', 'me', and 'you' (identity) helps children to understand that what they do influences how things will be in the future.

Not only can they sit, crawl and walk, but they can also run and jump on two legs together. What they do causes other people to react in different ways, so that they can cause anger or laughter, are swept up into someone's arms out of the way of danger, or are cuddled when upset.

They are developing a sense of self. This means that they are beginning to understand that they are different from other people, with their own unique body, feelings, thoughts and ideas, and friends and loved ones. Understanding other people is another way in which children go beyond themselves into more abstract thinking.

It takes three years or so to work all this out. Moving on from being a toddler is a huge transformation. We can see the scale of change if we study the child's play during this time of transition.

CHILDREN DEVELOP IMAGINATION FROM IMAGES IN THEIR MINDS

Imaginative people can think beyond the way things are. They can transform images into new ideas, feelings and relationships. When they process these images in their brains to make new images, they are imagining.

Babies and toddlers are able to form images. How else could they remember faces?

Images help humans to move from existing entirely in the here and now (the present) into the past and future. It is easier to remember a face you have seen before (in the past) than it is to see a face and then anticipate what the person will do next (in the future).

So, images are central to being able to imagine. Objects can contribute too. Seeing a spoon helps the baby to anticipate, and imagine a mealtime. 'Images' need not be visual – our brains can use sound and smell images to help us move beyond the present. Such images will be central to the imaginations of babies with a visual impairment, for example.

BEING ABLE TO IMITATE OTHERS HELPS CHILDREN TO RECONSTRUCT PAST EXPERIENCES IN NEW WAYS

Imitation is another important part of the process of moving out of the here and now, and of developing the possibility of thinking about the past or future.

OBSERVING A CHILD IMITATE

In the next photograph sequence, we can see how a two-year-old girl, Ella, has learnt some of the movements for playing with a ball by watching other people. She can imitate them.

Successful imitation involves two things.

1. There is the socio-cultural aspect, which influences what and who children imitate. Ella imitates people in her family who participate in football.

2. The other aspect of imitation is biological . In order to imitate people she has seen playing football, she must be sufficiently physically co-ordinated to throw the ball and catch it. She can throw the ball better than she can catch it. She has to manage as best she can. The more she tries to throw and catch, the more practised she will become.

Development and learning through play

BIOLOGICAL INFLUENCES

The biological possibility to throw and catch a ball is present within Ella. However, in order for it to emerge, she needs to play with a ball or, even better, to be helped by other people to play with the ball. Her biological structures (the ability to throw) are triggered by playing ball with an adult. She can then develop increasing skill through experience.

▲ Bit more practice needed for catching.

▲ Picking up the dropped catch.

▲ Preparing to throw – just like the grown-ups do it.

▲ Ready . . . steady . . .

▲ Go . . .

▲ Feeling triumphant after a great throw.

We need to look at the way nature (biological development) and nurture (socio-cultural development) have helped each other along so far in Ella's development. Through her play with objects and people, she has gained impressive mastery, and she still strives to develop further.

Her biological development has enabled her to pick up objects and throw them. This isn't as easy as it sounds. Some objects present more challenges than others in this respect. We need to look at what is involved, and how childhood play helps the process along.

- Sitting babies tend to be given objects and toys which are easy to hold in one hand, using a palmar grip.

- Crawlers begin to go and get objects they like the look of. The objects are not always easy to grasp or grip. This widens their world and challenges them (and adults living with them!)

- Toddlers love to hold an object in each hand, and to walk about with these. They frequently drop them, by accident, or on purpose, and put huge effort into picking them up.

- Small children, as they turn into steady walkers, love to carry things about. They transport things in their hands, but also in bags, baskets and wheeled vehicles that can be pushed along. They rarely sit still, and nor should they be made to! They cannot learn effectively if they cannot move (Goddard-Blythe, 2000). This is because to sit still requires huge effort for a young child, as they have to co-ordinate many different parts of their body in order to do so.

Ella, the little girl in the photographs, can throw the ball but catching it is difficult (Davies, 2001). She cannot yet aim where she throws the ball. She watches intently to see where it goes, and then smiles with pleasure. She runs across the grass, and puts out her arms, as if to feel the joy throughout her body (see page 53). Young children express emotion very strongly, they are consumed with joy, anger, love or fear.

She frequently uses her arms as wings, as if to develop her sense of balance. She is also learning to turn her body rapidly in spins, without falling over (see page 53).

Ella can clench her fists, and spread her fingers as she picks up the ball and throws it, or waits to catch it. At the moment, she always fails to catch the ball. However, she is imitating the way adults wait to receive a catch. She remains still, as if waiting for the ball to come to her. She has yet to anticipate where it will land, and run to meet it.

▲ Running with joy, arms out.

▲ Spinning takes balance and concentration.

▲ Developing a sense of balance.

This is because she still thinks in separate images. She still thinks in the present. Her thinking is becoming more mobile, but it has yet to transform images into moving thoughts which will help her consider the past and future with ease. When she has mastered the transformation, she will be able to anticipate (think of the future) where the ball will land.

Biologically, she needs to practise gripping, releasing, spreading her hands, reaching for objects, and working out how to get hold of them when they move. It is difficult to function as an adult without being able to do these things. All of these actions are part of preparing a meal, riding a bike, crossing a road with a pram, doing the shopping, replacing a light bulb.

In their play, children practise these actions in safety. Ella returns again and again to throw the ball, asking the adults to throw it back to her.

▲ Playing again and again – Ella feels safe enough to practise and make mistakes.

Now Ella is learning to stroke the cat gently (see page 55). This is a real challenge. She has to bend and keep her balance, and anticipate the movement of the cat. She advances with her hand spread out. She moves into a play mode, but she does not yet have the mastery and competence of gentle stroking to keep the cat from running off. She is not yet ready to play with the cat.

▲ Learning to be gentle with the cat.

▲ The cat might stay to play when she has learned to be gentle.

▲ Practising being gentle.

At this stage, it is easier for her to bend and point her finger into the water than to play with the cat. She does this gently. She does not have to worry about the water's emotions! The water is not like the cat. It does not run away if she is not gentle enough!

SOCIO-CULTURAL INFLUENCES

Ella's play is deeply influenced by the socio-cultural aspects of her life. Her father is Italian, and her mother is English. The extended family often gather in the family restaurant for meals together. Ella is relaxed about meeting people she doesn't know well.

She comes to the door to greet me, a visitor, with a letter in her hand and gives it to me, saying, 'Daddy.' She points to the writing on the envelope. Her mother has told her the letter is addressed to her father.

Her way of getting to know me seems to be to show me one of her books, and then an adult book. Next she does roly-polies on the floor, which are quite dance-like.

It is fascinating to see how she finds it difficult to open her book. This is because, although she has the palmar movement in her hands, the pincer movement (co-ordination of finger and thumb) is still developing. Whilst she is doing this, she is not playing but struggling to get the book open.

▲ Struggling to open the book.

She is a typical two-year-old, in that she doesn't want help. She wants to do it herself, even if she can't! Fortunately, on this occasion all is well, and she manages it after a struggle. Two-year-olds often become very frustrated. They know what they want to do, because they are beginning to be more mobile in their thinking – they can imagine what they want to happen. They have an image of what the book will look like when it is open. *But* their bodies are not as co-ordinated as they need them to be in order to make this happen.

Once she has got the book open, she begins to play at being a reader. Her intense look changes into smiles, and her body is

▲ Managing to get it open.

more relaxed. She shows off everything she knows about reading a book. She points at the pictures, and tells the colours (see below). She manages to turn the page with style. She knows books have to be the right way up in order to see the pictures.

Ella is very much in a state of transition from her toddler times. She still loves to hold or touch a different object with each hand. She points at the pictures in another book with one hand, and holds a bowl of snacks in the other (see page 60).

She puts the bowl down in order to turn the page of the book, which takes huge concentration and effort, and several attempts (see page 61).

▲ Playing at being a reader.

▲ Pointing with one hand and holding with the other.

She leaves the book aside when she puts the bowl on the table, and takes a snack to eat from it. She is co-ordinating objects and her movements as she plays at being a reader. She delights in having company while she does all of this.

Key

Biological and socio-cultural influences

Both the biological and the socio-cultural strands of development influence the possibility of children learning deeply through their play.

Each has an impact on the way that children are able to transform their images, and imitate people and what they do, so that they are increasingly able to think in the past, present and future.

▲ Turning pages takes both hands.

USING THE 12 FEATURES OF PLAY IN THE ANALYSIS

The 12 features of play

1. *Using first-hand experiences*
2. *Making up rules*
3. *Making props*
4. *Choosing to play*
5. *Rehearsing the future*
6. *Pretending*
7. *Playing alone*
8. *Playing together*
9. *Having a personal agenda*
10. *Being deeply involved*
11. *Trying out recent learning*
12. *Co-ordinating ideas, feelings and relationships for free-flow play*

(Adapted from Bruce 1991, 1996)

- Because she is only in the third year of her life, she still needs plenty of first-hand experiences, out of which she will build her play so that she can move beyond the here and now. We have seen her initiate relating to people, play with a book, do roly polies on the floor, throw and try to catch a ball, try to play with the cat, and to touch the water. (Feature 1.)

- Like the toddler in Chapter 4, Ella makes up her own little sequences as she plays. These sequences are her own rules, which she applies over and over again with the ball, or the book. She keeps control of what she does, and will not tolerate interference in this from anyone. At the moment she uses these rules as an unalterable sequence. She cannot transform her images and change them about. Play will open up the possibility to do this. (Feature 2.)

- She uses anything that comes to hand as a play prop, but she doesn't make her own yet. Play props help her to remember back to images in her mind and to give her prompts about what to do next as she begins to think forward. The football helps her to move like her image of a person playing football. The book helps her act as if she can read. (Feature 3.)

- She chooses whether to play or not. She is really in the mood to play at this time. She is like the baby and toddler in that she would not be able or willing to play if she felt uncomfortable, hungry or tired. This afternoon, she has had a sleep after coming home from her daycare group, and she is all set to play. (Feature 4.)

- Role play does not appear on this afternoon. She is rehearsing herself as a reader and football player, but she is not yet taking on the role of being someone else. (Feature 5.)

- She is not pretending yet. This process develops as the child becomes a symbol-user. She is already interested in the symbols of her culture. She wants to play football, and she wants to read. Symbols are a way of making one thing stand for another. At the moment, she is using the ball and the book to stand for doing what adults do, that is play football and read books.
  This kind of play will help her into more abstract thinking. Then she will be able to pretend all kinds of things in her play. (Feature 6.)

- She will now play alone at times, but only if a trusted adult is near. (Feature 7.)

- She loves to play with other children, and with adults. When she is at home, she expects to lead her own play. This allows her to use to the full the images she has from her past experience of football and books. When adults impose their images on a child's play, the play cannot develop as easily; it is constrained. When adults encourage the child's images, by supporting and extending them, they deepen the play. (Feature 8.)

■ She was eager to play with an adult. She was very clear that she wanted to play with the ball, and to look at books, and to roly poly on the floor. Her play agenda is beautifully strong. Her play agenda fits well with her biological need to develop hand control and to be able to co-ordinate her rotating or bending body. (Feature 9.)

■ She wallows in her play. She concentrates deeply in the different play episodes. (Figure 10.)

■ She is trying out her latest learning as she plays. She can throw a ball, pose ready to catch a ball, balance as she bends, balance as she twirls, and use the movements of a reader, pointing and naming, page turning, and holding the book. She shows both her biological and socio-cultural competencies as she plays. (Feature 11.)

■ Through her play, she co-ordinates what she knows about grip, release, watching where moving objects go, balance, rotation, how adults behave when they read or get ready to catch a ball. She is developing what she needs in order to anticipate her own movement in relation to a ball, or what she needs to do to become a reader. This helps her to go beyond the here and now. (Feature 12.)

Ella shows most of the 12 features in her play. She has yet to develop those which involve her in abstract thinking, that is being a symbol-user in a world of pretend and role play.

Summary

During the first three years, children develop a sense of their identity. They work out the concepts of 'I', 'me' and 'you'. This helps them to go beyond themselves in their ideas, feelings and relationships.

Beginning to talk in words or signs helps this process along.

Being able to think in images, to reconstruct the past and imagine the future, means they begin to move away from living mainly in the present.

They imitate things as they happen, but they also reconstruct what they saw people do on previous occasions, such as play football, or read a book.

Gradually, their thinking happens less and less in separate images. Images become transformed, and can be changed and altered during the thinking. Play helps this more flowing process of imaging to develop.

Children begin to develop play scenarios rehearsing adult roles, pretending, and finding and making play props. They become symbols-users.

Play helps toddlers to move from the here and now, and so they can think in more abstract ways which increasingly involve the past and the future.

6

Observing, supporting and extending play (toddlers and young children)

· · · · · · · · · · ·

Making friends with adults and children

In the previous chapters, we have looked at three children playing in the context of their homes. In this chapter, we shall consider some of the ways in which children growing up in the UK are supported and helped to make friends, and to deepen their play with others, both at home and in group settings.

Children vary in the ease with which they feel relaxed with people who are new to them. Some babies are very cuddly, and enjoy being held and passed to different people. Others are more reserved. Our personalities are affected by these aspects of our temperaments throughout our lives.

We need to respect children's feelings, as we help them to feel comfortable about widening the circle of adults and children that they play with.

PARENTS SUPPORTING PLAY IN THE HOME

In the next set of photographs, Jake is three years old. He is shy about meeting visitors in his home (see page 66).

He goes to stand by his mother. She moves to sit on the floor near some toys that she knows he likes. He joins her and sits on her lap (see page 66).

Jake hides behind her and she gradually talks to him about his cars (see page 67).

After a while, he settles and begins to play with them (see page 68).

▲ Feeling shy.

▲ Feeling more secure on mum's lap.

▲ Looking to mum for reassurance.

▲ Hiding.

▲ Talking to mum and feeling more settled.

▲ Relaxed enough to play.

It would be pointless to try and encourage Jake to concentrate and play until he feels relaxed enough to do so. No-one can concentrate and do their best learning if they are tense.

His mother is aware that he needs some support in getting settled. She moves from sitting on the chair, to sitting on the floor, so that she can be at his level. This does reassure him quite quickly. She can talk to the visitors, but also be physically very near him. When Jake wants her full attention, he can swivel on her lap and look at her face. Because she understands how he feels, and gently supports him by encouraging him to look at the cars, he soon becomes involved.

Once he is settled with his cars and is enjoying his play, he feels able to size up the visitors. He decides to show them his cars. He takes cars from the row he has made, and places them in a row near to the visitors. One visitor asks him about his cars, and he chats happily. His mother stays sitting quietly near him, so that he begins to make a relationship with the visitor.

Adults are very important to young children. This is because, in the context of the UK, they give children access strategies (Corsaro, 1979). Access strategies are ways of helping children to join each other's play.

Some social situations which adults and children alike might find difficult are:

- joining a group
- being joined by other people.

For example, you might have been invited to a party. You know the hosts, but none of their friends. You arrive on your own. What would help to make you feel comfortable?

Most people find it useful to be introduced to other guests by the host. This is because the host knows your interests and those of their other friends. They can be a useful bridge, helping you to find some common ground. For example, you and a fellow guest might both enjoy dancing, or photography.

Jake's mother knows that he takes time to feel relaxed when joined by newcomers. She knows he loves his toy cars. She knows he is helped when she is sitting near, or when he sits on her lap. She knows that, if she can get him started – in this case by sharing his interest with the newcomer visiting his home – she can remain seated near him on the floor, but withdraw enough to let him chat.

Parents helping to deepen play

In his play with cars, Jake loves to line them up and place them in a row. Jake is interested in which direction they are going, and talks about the driver being in front of or behind another car. He parks the cars in rows so that they are side by side, rather than one behind the other.

Jake is showing what he knows about lines. He demonstrates that he knows the difference between parallel lines (cars side by side) and lines which connect at crossroads, with right angles at the intersections. He does not yet have the words for this mathematical learning. This will come later, as he discusses these aspects with adults or older children who will be able to give him the words to go with his ideas.

Jake also knows about some aspects of space. He already has the mathematical language for this, as he talks about being in front or being behind.

Some access strategies for adults to help children settle

Children who feel churned up inside find it difficult to become settled enough to play. Adults who know the child can help by:

- letting the child stay near physically
- getting down to the child's level
- encouraging the child to look at their face, and keeping eye contact
- knowing the child's interests
- using what the child is interested in to help them settle
- staying physically near, but keeping quiet as the child begins to reach out and talk with other people.

(Whalley (ed) 2000)

You can see that Jake's mother was using all of these strategies. They are just as useful to adults in early years settings as they are to parents.

Settling children in group settings

RELAXING ENOUGH TO PLAY

Looking at the photograph below, it is easy to see which child is new to the group (actually in their first week), and which children are comfortably settled.

In Chapter 7 we shall see how Abigail, who is in the background looking at the autumn leaves and feels part of the group, begins to reach out and help this newcomer into play. But in this chapter we are concentrating on what adults can do to help children settle.

Joining a group is an emotional experience. The time it takes for different children to feel part of things – to feel able to play –

▲ Feeling confident enough to study leaves deeply, or feeling
a bit unsettled?

▲ Looking at leaves.

varies enormously. Other children help new children to settle, but adults are able to help children feel included in deep and important ways. Examples of things adults can do are:

- visiting the child and family before the child joins the group

- making sure a member of the family the child feels close to stays for the first fortnight or so, and withdraws gradually

- having something, such as a particular toy, in the group setting which the child is known to like

- supporting the child with access strategies (outlined above) so that the child gains confidence and joins in.

Key
Once children feel included, play begins to develop.

An example of outdoor play

Play should be supported both indoors and outdoors. This can be a challenge. In this early childhood group, the outdoor area is small. So the children are taken daily to the park to use the wider spaces, before returning to eat their lunch. Staff are committed to outdoor play, and their determination that this group of children experience its benefits is demonstrated in the way they structure the curriculum (QCA, 2000).

Autumn leaves make a natural play prop. Adults join in the play, running in the park with the children and enjoying the space. This group of children all live in an inner-city area of London. Only a few have gardens, and most live in flats. The need for well-planned outdoor play when they come to the group setting is, therefore, of central importance.

▲ Being still and thoughtful.

Play will always ebb and flow. There will be quiet still times and noisy boisterous times. It is quite difficult to sustain free-flow play (Bruce, 1991, 1996). So, regularly, children will peel off and

▲ Running with friends.

take a few minutes quietly doing sometime different before rejoining the group (see page 73). The children run about with friends, moving along in lines side by side, or following one another. Leaders emerge, who then become followers. There is awareness of others, but not much is said. There is a lot of quiet smiling and, from time to time, laughter. This opens children up to learning (Trevarthen, 1998).

Key

The ebb and flow of play enables children to develop naturally towards the following early learning goals.

Early Learning Goal

Physical development

QCA, 2000:108

Show awareness of space, of themselves and of others.

Early Learning Goal

Personal, social and emotional development

QCA, 2000:34

Have a developing awareness of their own needs, views and feelings and be sensitive to the needs, views and feelings of others.

This group of children demonstrate in their play that they can co-ordinate their movements together. This will be invaluable to them if, in their later schooling, they play music in a group, dance in a group, or become involved in drama improvisations. It will also be useful in playing team sports, such as football, netball or hockey.

In the photograph on page 72 the girl is looking intently at the leaves. The adult points out the difference between the dry leaf and the green leaf, and the patterns of the leaves. Quite naturally and within her play, the girl has satisfied some of the early learning goals (see below).

Early Learning Goal

Communication, language and literacy

QCA, 2000:58

Use talk to organise, sequence and clarify thinking, ideas, feelings and events.

Early Learning Goal

Mathematical development

QCA, 2000:80

Talk about, recognise and recreate simple patterns.

QCA, 2000:86

Investigate objects and materials by using all of their senses as appropriate.

Find out about, and identify, some features of living things, objects and events they observe.

How to support play in the Foundation Stage (3–6 years of age)

When people say children learn entirely through play, they are saying something highly inaccurate. Play is *central* to learning, but it is not the only way children learn. Children also learn by watching other children, observing adults, imitating what they see, through their senses, by joining in games like snakes and ladders, through first-hand experiences like cooking and through teaching.

Staff in early childhood group settings need to organise the day so that the natural ebb and flow of play episodes and scenarios can be supported. If children are not free to pace their play, the quality of play drops. Children need to intersperse their intense free-flow play with some of these other ways of learning, and with rest. But if children are always in situations where adults control what they do, they become constrained in their learning.

Childhood play will turn into adult creativity and imagination, but only if it is encouraged. It can be extinguished or diminished if it is not supported or extended.

When adults provide a varied play environment with opportunities to learn in all the different ways, they enable children to achieve some of the early learning goals.

Early Learning Goal

Creative development

QCA, 2000:126

Respond in a variety of ways to what they see, hear, smell, touch and feel.

The most important ways to support play are:

- to structure the environment, so that it is conducive to the occurrence of play and play is more likely to arise
- for an adult to take an interest, and be part of the play in a background way
- for the adult to be sensitive and aware of how to help things along without taking over.

Curriculum Guidance for the Foundation Stage (QCA, 2000)

The three bullet points on page 76 arise out of:

1. the traditional heritage of the pioneers of early childhood education in the UK

2. evidence about the way children learn from research and theory.

The ideas in the bullet points are supported by the *Curriculum Guidance for the Foundation Stage* in England.

This document stresses the importance of:

- 'assessment' (= observation) of what children do

- planning stepping stones for children to develop towards the early learning goals in each of the six areas of learning; the stepping stones will be informed by the observations made of children's prior learning

- using the stepping stones to 'teach' (= observe, support and extend the learning of the children). Part of this teaching is to engage children in well-planned play, based on observations.

By observing children at play, adults can assess their learning in all six areas of the English Foundation Stage and plan the next stepping stones which will lead them towards the early learning goals.

The magic of teaching lies in creating the right stepping stones of learning for each individual child. Although we don't achieve this all the time, when we get it just right we know why we want to teach, and we say we've had a really good, deeply satisfying day.

Observing play is an invaluable tool for assessing, planning and teaching. It helps to develop well-planned play.

Teaching is about observing, supporting and extending play and all kinds of learning (Bruce, 1987).

SUPPORTING AN ACTIVITY — PLAYING SHOP

The group of children in the daycare setting shown in the following photographs have visited a local shop. A shop has been set up in the room, with play props. A table becomes the counter. Baskets are provided. Crockery is sold, and various bottles become pretend items. The children add to this, using their initiative as the play scenario develops.

Some of the children choose to play, and move into role with great skill. Two are shopkeepers, and others are customers.

▲ Setting up shop.

▲ Being a shopkeeper.

▲ The adult joins in from time to time to sustain and extend the play.

The adult supports the play by becoming a customer. This role modelling encourages other children to take a turn at being a customer. Once again, as in the outside play, children join the play, and leave it for a short break doing something else, only to return for more of the play scenario.

There is plenty of chatter about the cost of items of shopping, and putting them in bags. The play was sustained for nearly an hour before it faded. The adult sat on the edge of the play, and became different characters buying goods from the shopkeepers.

Linking what adults do to the Curriculum Guidance

- The adults assess/observe the shop play (what the children do).

- This informs the way they plan stepping stones for children.

- The stepping stones will take the children on their journey towards the early learning goals. They will be used as the basis of direct and indirect teaching.

The **Curriculum Guidance for the Foundation Stage** *(QCA, 2000:22) says that ꞌ Teaching means systematically helping children to learn, so that they are helped to make connections in their learning and are actively led forward, as well as helped to reflect on what they have already learnt. ꞌ*

Extending play – getting the balance right

One of the most important things about extending play is not to overstructure it . If adults lead the play all the time, the child's imagination and creativity will shut down.

On the other hand, leaving children entirely without help to extend their play means the imagination and creativity that might have developed does not develop. This is because children don't know enough about how to free-flow play imaginatively.

Play doesn't always just happen. It needs people who help it along.

Well-planned play means developing the skill to support and extend play, informed by careful observation.

PLANNING THE STEPPING STONES

For children who role play easily, the adult can support the children in developing a story through the play scenario of a shop. Some early learning goals will be covered on the way.

Early Learning Goal

Communication, language and learning

QCA, 2000:50

Listen with enjoyment, and respond to stories, songs and other music, rhymes and poems and *make up their own stories*, songs, rhymes and poems.

Early Learning Goal

Creative development

QCA, 2000:124

Use their imagination in art and design, music, dance, *imaginative and role play and stories*.

Through the shop-play scenario adults can provide appropriate stepping stones for these children. The play environment can be carefully structured to encourage role play. Creating stories requires children to create characters and a story line (narrative). But the children cannot write down their stories yet. Neither are they ready for adults to write down their stories, because they are only just learning what is involved in making a story. The shop-play scenario will give them a stepping stone towards this. It takes years of practice making play scenarios before rich stories are written down by the child.

Planning different stepping stones for the different needs and interests of different children

For the children who are paying attention to costs of items, the shop-play provision can emphasise number. The weighing machine, cash register, price labels, price list, coins and cheque books all give opportunities to explore number. Some children will address early learning goals in this way.

Early Learning Goal

Mathematical development

QCA, 2000:74

Say and use number names in order in familiar contexts.

Count reliably up to 10 everyday objects.

Recognise numerals 1 to 9.

For the children who are interested in making things, cutting paper to the right size for wrapping items or making a shop window display might help them into the play scenario, especially if they do not usually enjoy this kind of play. Again, they will be developing towards early learning goals through their play.

Early Learning Goal

Knowledge and understanding of the world

QCA, 2000:90

Select the tools and techniques they need to shape, assemble and join material they are using.

Selecting the right size bag, or cutting and joining the grease proof paper to wrap the cheese or bacon can give children stepping stones towards another goal.

Early Learning Goal

Creative development

QCA, 2000:124

Use their imagination in *art and design*, music, dance, imaginative and role play and stories.

Indirect teaching is powerful

It is important to ensure the stepping stones towards early learning goals that we provide utilise both direct and indirect teaching strategies.

What is teaching?

Our teaching grows out of our observations of individual children who we know well. It is when we enable them to learn.

For example, we may be watching a child who is struggling to use scissors. Perhaps their current inability to master cutting is holding back their play. We may demonstrate that it is easier to use scissors if we hold them in a certain way. This is *direct* teaching.

We may have observed another child who is already very good at using scissors. Perhaps we have observed that they have a particular interest in cutting different materials. We might decide to structure a play environment that would enable the child to explore their interest in depth. Perhaps a workshop or post office area would give them some exciting opportunities. This is *indirect* teaching.

Indirect teaching strategies are especially powerful, because they allow flexibility and encourage children to use initiative and be active learners. Indirect teaching strategies often lead to children reaching early learning goals that the adult had not intended to teach. This is very exciting, and makes teaching both fun and deeply satisfying. What could be better than to find that children have learnt more than you taught them!

An example could be that a child who finds it difficult to sit quietly and listen to a story enters into the role play. They are the customer 'in a rush to do the shopping'. By becoming involved in a way in which they are capable, the child 'maintains attention and concentrates'. In this shop-play scenario, therefore, the child has made a valuable step towards a learning goal.

Early Learning Goal

Personal, social and emotional

QCA, 2000: 32

Maintain attention, concentrate, and sit quietly when appropriate.

This child is much more likely to enjoy storytime with the group after plenty of experience making up stories through play scenarios. In fact, the child is likely to use some of the ideas from stories they listen to in their play scenarios.

This kind of indirect teaching has a powerful effect on learning.

Practical ways to extend play

Key

There are two important aspects to extending free-flow play, and so developing well-planned play:

1. *extending the provision*

2. *things adults do.*

EXTENDING THE PROVISION

Having made a basic shop for the children to play with, adults can extend the provision based on what they have observed has already taken the children's interest. For example, perhaps:

■ the bags and baskets are well used

■ so are the objects for sale

■ the children pretend to use money.

Leading on from these observations, we could make some or all of the following changes to our provision.

■ There could be a variety of bags. Paper bags of different sizes could be offered and carrier bags provided (carefully supervised and never left unattended). Bags would be beautifully presented, perhaps hanging on a hook on the wall, or in neat boxes on the counter. Children could choose a bag to put their shopping in.

■ There could be a weighing machine, and a balance. Although children do not yet understand the calibrations on such equipment, they benefit from learning that it helps us to know how heavy something is. They might pick out numbers. They will understand more easily later on that the arm of the balance will be straight if two things are the same weight.

Although they do not understand the concept of weight yet, they do have a sense of balance and symmetry. This will help them to develop a concept of weight in the long term. Play is an important vehicle for reflecting on such things without pressure to perform.

It looks as if children are just messing about with balances and weighing machines, but they are experimenting and exploring, musing on things in ways which will build into higher concepts, such as weight and number.

■ A cash machine could be made out of a box. Coins could be made out of cardboard. When adults make play props, they are being good role models for creativity. Children can be encouraged to add their props too. For example, one child might pick up a piece of card and 'swipe' it over the counter. They have created a credit card.

■ Children might enjoy being shop assistants who have to put prices on the articles for sale, or bar codes. Having some sticky labels could be very exciting.

■ Having a price list – with a picture of each object for sale and a price next to it – encourages children to play with numbers. This could be in the form of a book, or on a piece of stiff cardboard.

■ There could be a window display in the shop. A child who wants to be part of the play, but who needs to be alone in the play scenario might find this a good way to join in. They would need drapes and perhaps torches to spotlight the objects on display.

■ The objects for sale could be extended. Many children play at supermarkets as this tunes into their experiences. Empty packets of cereal, stuffed with newspaper to keep the shape, and pretend tins of food in the shape of cylinders are popular. These can be made from offcuts of wood. Some children might enjoy drawing pictures on them (felt pens are good for this) to show the food that is in the pretend tin. Older children might enjoy making labels from rectangles of paper, drawing pictures of the food and then sticking them on the cylinder. But this requires considerable skill, and is not easy for children in the Foundation years (3–6 years). It would be an enjoyable extension for children in Key Stage 2 of the English System (7–11 years).

- Foods such as cheese can be made using dough. Children enjoy using wire-cutters to cut the pretend cheese, and placing it on greaseproof paper or polythene sheets to be weighed.

  They can also make fruit and vegetables, fish and meat out of the dough. There might be a table or workshop area near to the shop where children could do this. They could even play out a scenario at a bread factory. Buns, rolls, bread, biscuits and cakes could be set out on trays to be taken from the factory to the shop.

- Some children might enjoy transporting the goods from the factory and delivering them to the shop using a cart and pretending to drive it.

- Some children might enjoy dressing up as the different characters who visit the shop. So, having a dressing up corner near the shop would be helpful. Adults might need to role model this, and pretend to be a customer coming to the shop. Children might appreciate realistic paper hats to wear when serving at the cheese counter.

Some very important issues are emerging from our consideration of the play provision.

- Children will not extend into rich, free-flow play unless they are helped to do so, because it is too difficult. Play leads them into abstract thinking, which is not easy to do.

- Therefore, adults need to join the play.

- They need to join the play in ways which do not take it over, but which help the children to become as independent in their play as possible.

- Children who extend their play have their own ideas, play out their own feelings, and explore the relationships they have with others. They are not dependent on adults for their thinking. They become autonomous learners, who can get on with learning without waiting for adults to tell them what to do, think, feel, or how to relate to others. They are in control, and able to learn in deep ways in their play.

- Children are helped to extend their play if they have play props, but the play props need to be open to an imaginative response. Commercially made props have very limited value, and they are expensive. They only encourage a narrow response from children. A plastic apple is usually played with as if it is an apple. A child can make whatever fruit or vegetable they want with a lump of dough!

■ Props made by the children to serve their imaginative and creative ideas, feelings and relationships with others are richer than any other kind of prop for extending play.

■ Some children do not have to rely on props very much at all. They can pretend, and often use mime and movement, for example to pretend pouring tea into an imaginary cup.

HOW ADULTS CAN EXTEND THE PLAY

Adults playing with young children will use one of four strategies. Sometimes they are conscious of these, and sometimes not. Adults who are informed about the way children develop find it easier to extend play than those who are not.

Most adults rely on remembering their own childhood play, and passing on what they learnt about it as children to the next generation. There will be a huge cultural dimension in this. Some adults will have learnt about play from adults. Others will have learnt about it from other children.

Interest and imitation

Two common strategies are shown by the photograph on page 87.

1. Some adults might simply be there, and look interested. Children are then highly likely to draw them into the play.

2. They might imitate what the experienced player does.

In the photograph the adult on the left has used the first strategy. The child is now spontaneously showing her the soft toy.

The adult in the centre of the photograph is using the second strategy, and is imitating the child who is dressing the doll.

By invitation

A third strategy for extending play is to just be there, but not taking an obvious interest unless invited. This is important if the child moves into free-flow play, needing privacy and to be left uninterrupted. These moments of flow are deep for the child, and may be quite fleeting or of sustained length. This is where adults

▲ The two adults are each using a different strategy to become involved in the play.

need to be very sensitive, and able to tune into the child's play needs.

In the photograph on page 88, the child is pretending to talk on the telephone. Because he is imagining what the person on the other end is saying, it would be very frustrating if an adult started to join the play. What he is doing is very sophisticated. This is rich free-flow play when considered in terms of the 12 features of play.

▲ Playing freely and alone.

USING THE 12 FEATURES OF PLAY IN THE ANALYSIS

Key

The 12 features of play

1. *Using first-hand experiences*

2. *Making up rules*

3. *Making props*

4. *Choosing to play*

5. *Rehearsing the future*

6. *Pretending*

7. *Playing alone*

8. *Playing together*

9. *Having a personal agenda*

10. *Being deeply involved*

11. *Trying out recent learning*

12. *Co-ordinating ideas, feelings and relationships for free-flow play*

(Adapted from Bruce 1991, 1996)

In his play with the telephone, the boy is:

■ using his experience of telephones (Feature 1)

■ making up his own rules of how a conversation goes (Feature 2)

■ using the phone as a play prop (Feature 3)

■ playing spontaneously. No-one told him to do it (Feature 4)

■ rehearsing the way adults behave (Feature 5)

■ pretending to have a conversation with an imaginary person (Feature 6)

■ playing alone (Feature 7)

■ developing his personal agenda for play (which is having telephone conversations) (Feature 9)

■ deeply involved; when children are wallowing in their play, they should not be disturbed by outside influences, such as adults asking them questions (Feature 10)

■ showing his skill in how to use a telephone (Feature 11)

■ able to bring together in a way which makes sense for him, what he knows about telephones and what they are for (Feature 12).

Conversation

A fourth and important strategy for extending play is through conversations with children. For example, in the shop play (see pages 77–79), the adult pretends to buy provisions. An important aspect of play is that it should be clear to everyone playing what the play scenario is about. This means that everyone who wants to join in can. The play scenario's theme usually begins with an 'announcement'. A child might say, 'Let's play shops.' This gives a play theme that children can join in with, or not, as they wish. There is no reason why an adult should not make an 'announcement' and offer a play scenario scene. The adult might say something like, 'I'm going to play shopping.'

Once the play scenario has a theme which everyone knows about, the adult can say something like, 'I am going to be the Mum, so I'm going to put on my hat because it's cold outside.' Children are likely to join in. Hopefully, they will begin to voice *their* play agenda, and develop their ideas. As this begins to happen, the adult can hold back more and more, staying in the background unless needed. The more the adult is needed in the play scenario, the lower the level of play will be.

The play might look quite exciting to an outsider, because the adult will be making up a good story line (a narrative) about shopping. The adult will be helping children to move into their roles pretending to be shop-keepers, or customers, or factory workers, or delivery people. The adult might be helping children to stay in role, so that they stay in the character for a sustained time. *But*, if it all depends on the adult, then it only shows that the adult can engage children in rich free-flow play. It does not mean that the children can manage it on their own.

The aim of the adult should be – not to withdraw from the play, because staying in the play shows that adults value it – to take an increasingly backstage part in it.

ADULTS AS CATALYSTS FOR FREE-FLOW PLAY

Adults need to become play catalysts, rather than keeping children dependent on them in their play.

If free-flow play is encouraged, then children are likely to turn into good creative story writers in middle childhood. This is because they will know:

- how to create a character
- how to develop the character's adventures
- how to create an interesting story, and take it to the end
- how to make the different characters interact with each other.

Early Learning Goal

Communication, language and literacy

QCA, 2000:62

Show an understanding of the elements of stories, such as main character, sequence of events, and openings.

Getting into role is a real challenge. This is why play props and dressing up clothes are so helpful. Looking like or feeling like the character helps. Pretending to be everyday people is easier than trying to be a spaceman, superhero or heroine (Holland, 1999). This is because children can use their real life experience to base the character on, e.g. Daddy washing up.

The adult can help the child, once he or she is dressed up and ready to play perhaps not knowing how to start play flowing, by getting the two characters to talk to each other. The adult, who is pretending to be the Mum, might say something like, 'I've got to buy some potatoes today. My children keep wanting chips for supper. Do your children ask you for their favourite meals?' The child can then reply in the role of neighbour, but with plenty of opportunities to develop their own ideas.

In this chapter, we have looked at how adults can both support play, and extend it into the highest levels of free-flow play. When adults observe, support and extend children's learning through well-planned play, they are teaching.

Summary

The Curriculum Guidance for the Foundation Stage in England (QCA, 2000) defines teaching as:

Systematically helping children to learn so that they are helped to make connections in their learning and are actively led forward, as well as helped to reflect on what they have already learnt.

Well-planned play helps children in all of these ways. It is a central teaching strategy for the Foundation Years.

This approach to teaching builds on the heritage of the pioneers of the early childhood curriculum, which has become evidence based and is now supported by research and theory. All 12 of the features of play are supported and extended by teaching, but adults can be especially powerful in developing feature 12. Nothing else in the early childhood curriculum supports this feature so effectively.

Feature 12

Children at play co-ordinate their ideas, feelings and make sense of relationships with their family, friends and culture. When play is co-ordinated it flows along in a sustained way. It is called free-flow play (Bruce, 1991).

7

How play helps children to understand other people

Childhood play enables children to be at their best. Well-planned play gives children the stepping stones they need to develop towards the early learning goals in all areas of learning in the English Foundation Stage.

Learning about good and bad

As they deepen their play, they become philosophers, struggling with what is good and what is evil. They reflect on what makes people kind, and what it means to treat people with fairness. Are you a baddie if you didn't *mean* to hurt someone? Do you become a baddie if you meant to do harm? How do other people react to kindness? What should people do if others cheat them, hit them, trick them, or help them? All of these philosophical themes, exploring morality and justice, are in childhood play.

The themes which children develop in their play scenarios contribute to their personal, social and emotional development.

Early Learning Goal

Personal, social and emotional development

QCA, 2000:38

Understand what is right and what is wrong, and why. Consider the consequences of their words and actions for themselves and others.

Of course, we go on trying to work out what is right or wrong for all of our lives. Right and wrong can be one of the most difficult distinctions to make.

Learning about feelings

Feelings run deep in play. The great themes of literature across the world are played out: there are sad and joyful meetings and partings, terrifying and daring raids; there are situations which involve creeping up on people and surprising them, operating in gangs, being abandoned, being caught, being rescued and being helped and protected. All of this is very emotional, but it also contributes to an understanding of story.

Early Learning Goal

Communication, language and literacy

QCA, 2000:62

Show an understanding of the elements of stories, such as main character, sequence of events, and openings...

Coping with life

In their play, children face the difficulties of their lives. They deal with their feelings. They find ways of coping with situations or people that hurt their feelings, or make them angry. They come to terms with their lives, or find ways of changing them as they experiment in their play with different ways of relating to people.

Childhood play helps children to learn that different people have different ideas. It helps them to get inside other people's heads, feelings and relationships.

Observing empathy overcome anxiety

Every child who attends a group setting has experienced being new in the group. They know how it feels to be with people you don't yet know well, and to wonder how they will treat you. They may have had positive experiences, where they have been gently introduced to the way the group works, in an atmosphere of warmth and affection. They may have been helped to make friends. In this case, they might enjoy helping a new child by doing the same for them.

On the other hand, they may have felt anxious, having to find their own way into the group, copying what the other children

▲ Deeply interested in cars.

do in order to learn how things are done, and in the hope of making some friends. It might have been hard not to feel unsettled, sad and lonely, and even frightened at times.

In the photograph above, we can see two boys playing with cars. They are watched by another boy (see page 95).

It is this little boy's first week in the group. An adult, who cannot be seen in the photographs, is sitting behind him. Later on, we shall see how the newcomer has chosen to be near the boy in the blue-striped top. At this point in the morning, the older boy is not aware that he is needed by the younger child. He is deeply involved in the play with his friend.

The three boys are each developing towards the same early learning goal (see page 96), but they will each need different stepping stones.

■ **The newcomer is beginning to learn about forming good relationships by watching experienced players and role models.**

▲ Exploring movement on slopes and how wheels fit into grooves, unaware of being watched.

▲ Taking turns and talking about what happens, still being observed from the sidelines.

▲ Watching the play, still not quite ready to join in.

■ The experienced players are developing agreed values, codes of behaviour and are working together harmoniously.

■ All three children need time to play with cars, so that they can develop their play in ways appropriate for them.

Early Learning Goal

Personal, social and emotional development

QCA, 2000:36

Work as part of a group or class, taking turns and sharing fairly, understanding that there needs to be agreed values and codes of behaviour for groups of people, including adults and children, to work together harmoniously.

At the end of every morning, the children go to the park. This is a big moment for the new child, who has been trying to feel at home in the secure setting of the room. The adults are careful to make sure that he is looked after, explaining where they are going and what they will do (see page 97).

▲ Explaining about the park.

Once he is in the park, he is not sure what to do. He uses a well tried way of coping. If in doubt, do what everyone else is doing (see page 98). The other children are looking up at the trees. This is because an adult has suggested that the leaves were on the trees, but are falling because it is autumn. Yet, he is obviously not yet feeling part of the group.

Some of the children set off for a run towards some trees on the other side of the grass. The boy he wanted to sit near – the one who was playing with the cars with his friend – calls to him to follow (see page 98). He does.

It is as if the older boy is signalling that he knows how it feels to be new, and is trying to make him feel part of the group (see page 99). This is empathy. Empathy involves understanding how someone else feels and being able to put yourself in their shoes.

▲ Copying the others but not quite fitting in.

▲ An invitation to join in.

▲ Feeling empathy with the newcomer.

However, there is something else which play helps children to develop, something that is more sophisticated than empathy and that develops out of it. This is a theory of mind. It means that children begin to be able to recognise that you might think or feel differently about something from me, as we saw briefly in the Introduction.

It may be that, when the older boy was settling into the group, he wanted to be with an adult all the time for the first week or two, before venturing to do things with the other children. It seems that this newcomer is different. From the beginning, he seeks out an older child, who is well established in the group, to follow. The older boy seems to have recognised this, by calling to him to join in. If we were to ask him about it, he probably would be unaware of what he had done.

The newcomer follows his new friend, but looks a little lost. This is noticed by one of the girls, who smiles at him, and leads him over to be near the older boy (see page 100).

▲ Approaching the newcomer with a smile.   ▲ Leading him to be with the older boy.

The older boy holds his hand, and takes the newcomer with him as he gathers leaves. He respects the fact that the newcomer doesn't want to pick up the leaves, as he is wishing to do (see below).

▲ Holding hands with the newcomer.   ▲ Gathering leaves while the newcomer watches.

So, both the older boy and the girl have empathy for the newcomer. They have also developed theory of mind. They understand that he needs to settle into the group in a *different way to the way that was right for them.*

▲ Playing with leaves.

Playing with autumn leaves in the park has given the children opportunities to use what they know about theory of mind. They are also developing towards a related early learning goal.

Early Learning Goal

QCA, 2000:34

Personal, social and emotional development

Have a developing awareness of their own needs, views and feelings and be sensitive to the needs, views and feelings of others.

The boy leader and girl leader are using their play in the park to experience and explore these issues. The newcomer is doing so in relation to the first part of the goal (developing an awareness of *his own* needs, views and feelings).

So, playing in the park with autumn leaves provides different stepping stones which are right for different children.

Key

As ever, play enables children to demonstrate their highest levels of learning.

Playing in pairs

In the photographs of the two boys playing with the cars (see pages 94–96), we see that they are constantly having to adjust to each other's play agenda . They need to be fine tuned to each other's thinking and feelings. If they aren't, then the play will fade. Neither of them wants that to happen, they are enjoying it so much. They want to keep the play free flowing along. Their pleasure in this play is not simply jolly fun. It is deeper than that. As they play together with the cars, they have adventures with ideas which are stimulating and exciting.

- They confirm their belief that cars go down slopes. One day they will use the word gravity.

- They see that a slope breaks a fall, so that the cars do not crash to the ground, but move along gently from a height to the roof of the trailer.

- They see how the groove on the ramp stops the cars from falling off as they travel downwards. These grooves are different from the train rails that keep trains on a track. The car wheels slot *into* the grooves on the trailer. The wheels on the train have grooves that slot *over* the train tracks. These sorts of things fascinate children. They may seem to be tiny details, but they embody important scientific concepts for young children to explore.

- As they play together, they are working out how the other is thinking and feeling. They are trying to understand each other. They find that, if they take turns, it goes well.

- They find that they both have a similar play agenda. Probably, each boy would like to have all the turns, but they have both worked out that, if they did that, it wouldn't be much fun for the other person who might leave the play.

- They are willing to give up doing exactly as they want and to think about what the other person wants, because the other person has good ideas that make the play go deeper.

■ If they use each other's ideas, they develop a better play scenario.

■ In order to develop rich, co-operative play, children need to be aware of how other children are thinking and feeling. They need to recognise that someone may have similar ideas but that someone else might have very different ideas.

The practitioners working with these boys might find it appropriate to help them develop towards the following early learning goals using their car play as a stepping stone. It is an ideal opportunity to initiate a train-play scenario.

Early Learning Goal

Knowledge and understanding of the world

QCA, 2000:86

Investigate objects and materials by using all of their senses as appropriate.

Early Learning Goal

Personal, social and emotional development

QCA, 2000:34

Have a developing awareness of their own needs, views and feelings and be sensitive to the needs, views and feelings of others.

Early Learning Goal

Personal, social and emotional development

QCA, 2000:36

Form good relationships with adults and peers.

Work as part of a group or class, taking turns and sharing fairly, understanding that there needs to be agreed values and codes of behaviour for groups of people, including adults and children, to work together harmoniously.

It is very important to note that adults working with young children in the Foundation Years should create their own stepping stones for children, and encourage children to develop their own. The stepping stones in the *Curriculum Guidance for the Foundation Stage* are offered as *examples* to give practitioners an idea of how they should go about this. They are *not* intended to be followed in an exact way, because they would not be based on observations of the children in the setting or childminder's home.

Children's roles in play

CHILDREN WHO LEAD THE PLAY

Children who are leaders in play are well developed in their understanding and awareness of others. In fact, if we observe closely, we find that the boy wearing the blue-striped top is leading the free-flow play scenario with the toy cars. In the park, he also showed awareness and understanding of the child who was new to the group. In both cases he is careful not to dominate the play. He makes all the suggestions about what to do, but he makes sure that his friend has plenty of turns with the cars, and feels as if he is actively participating.

There is a difference between *dominating* and *leading* the play.

The boy in the blue-striped top is definitely leading the play. This is because he has both *empathy and theory of mind* (POST, 2000).

Empathy

This is recognising how someone else feels, because you have similar feelings. It means you know how you would like to be treated. This links with the expression that we should always try to 'do as you would be done by'.

Theory of mind

This is recognising that someone feels and thinks differently from the way you do. A child who has theory of mind can work out how to develop the play with a partner, or even with a whole group.

Free-flow play is an invaluable preparation for adult life, because it enables children to develop theory of mind.

USING THE 12 FEATURES OF PLAY IN THE ANALYSIS

> ### Key
>
> *The 12 features of play*
>
> 1. *Using first-hand experiences*
> 2. *Making up rules*
> 3. *Making props*
> 4. *Choosing to play*
> 5. *Rehearsing the future*
> 6. *Pretending*
> 7. *Playing alone*
> 8. *Playing together*
> 9. *Having a personal agenda*
> 10. *Being deeply involved*
> 11. *Trying out recent learning*
> 12. *Co-ordinating ideas, feelings and relationships for free-flow play*
>
> *(Adapted from Bruce 1991, 1996)*

In the car play scenario, the boys are sharing what they know of scientific concepts. The world needs scientists who can lead teams of experts. The features they show in their play are as follows.

- They use their first-hand experience of cars and falling objects. (Feature 1.)
- They make up some rules for using the cars on the car transporter. (Feature 2.)
- They are using play props. (Feature 3.)
- They have chosen to play together, and when and how to play. (Feature 4.)
- They are playing in a pair. (Feature 8.)
- They respect each other's play agenda. (Feature 9.)
- They are deeply involved and wallow in their play. (Feature 10.)
- They are showing what they know about gravity, grooves, and breaking the fall of an object from a height. (Feature 11.)
- They are bringing together their ideas about these aspects of science. (Feature 12.)

The play with cars is not about rehearsing roles for adult life (Feature 5). Nor is it pretend play with props (Feature 6).

In the play scenario in the park, the older boy is again leading scientific enquiry. He is quietly leading other children into looking at fallen and green leaves, and making them into fans. In this play episode, he picks up the leaves in a bunch, with a dance like movement.

▲ Starting a play scenario.

The girl in the blue does the same. They move in synchrony, very aware of what the other is doing. He makes the play 'announcement' and shouts, 'I'm getting lots.' This encourages other children to join the play, and leaf gathering ripples through the group. Without any discussion, they follow their leader and hunt for the best leaves in this dance-like formation. Some of the ancient dances of the world involve people dancing in lines behind a leader. The children don't yet know about such things, but humans in every culture dance together.

In this free-flow play, the children are also demonstrating many of the 12 features.

- They use what they know about follow-my-leader formations. (Feature 1.)

- They have made a play rule that they will all look for leaves and follow the leader, without any discussion. (Feature 2.)

- They use the leaves as play props. (Feature 3.)

- No-one told them to do this. The play arose spontaneously. (Feature 4.)

- They are, without knowing it, rehearsing as future dancers. (Feature 5.)

- They are playing co-operatively. (Feature 8.)

- They use the play agenda of the boy leader who makes the play 'announcement'. They also use the play agenda of the girl leader, who signals everyone to respond to the play 'announcement' by joining in with his idea. (Feature 9.)

- They wallow in their play (except for the newcomer who tags along, giving it a try, and finding out how he feels about it). (Feature 10.)

- They use the skill they have developed in co-ordinating as a group in a large space, in ways which are like an improvised dance. (Feature 11.)

- The boy leader brings together his love of science (finding out about the different kinds of leaves) with dance-like movements in a group. (Feature 12.)

It is important to note that the adults were always near when this free-flow play got under way, but did not disturb it during the five minutes it lasted (see page 108). It suddenly faded and vanished, as free-flow play does. All the same, it is those magical few moments that we take with us through our lives, and which prepare us well for adulthood.

Key

Knowing about free-flow play and its features helps adults to develop well-planned play in the Foundation Stage, with appropriate stepping stones towards the early learning goals, in ways which are right for individual children.

NEWCOMERS TO PLAY

The newcomer is interested in what the boy leader, with the other children, is doing. He watches from the side, because he

▲ Adults are close by during the play.

does not yet feel comfortable about playing with leaves, or moving in synchrony with others in a dance-like way. He has yet to learn that play encourages children to make their own play props, to make up their own play rules, or pretend. It takes a bit of courage to join in if you are only just learning about these things. When you are new to a group, you are not likely to be at your most adventurous or courageous.

The practitioners working with him might decide to try to develop his confidence. They would be helping him towards an early learning goal.

Early Learning Goal

Personal, social and emotional development

QCA, 2000:32

Be confident to try new activities, initiate ideas, and speak in a familiar group.

His own self-selected stepping stone is watching others. They draw him into the play scenario in the park. His stepping stone is right for him. Adults make sure he feels included. He is trying something new, and when he feels secure enough he dares to do it. He is not yet ready to initiate play, or speak. This will be a later stepping stone, but it is too great a leap at the moment.

It is fascinating for this child to watch a confident player encouraging other children to join in. He likes to be near the boy leader. Perhaps this is because he has worked out that the boy is willing to help him into the play when he begins to feel ready for it. He also likes to be near the girl leader, and he dares to follow her in the line when she leads the other children into the play scenario. It won't be long before he feels able to join in and wallow in the play!

Key

If we want to produce children who are caring of others, able to lead and contribute to their own and other communities in a fast-changing world, we need to encourage free-flow play. It helps children to have empathy for others, and to respect the different ways that people think and feel.

CHILDREN WHO DOMINATE THE PLAY

Domination is very different from being a leader of the play scenario.

Children who dominate in group-play scenarios need adult help.

Maisie was four years old. She avoided any situation where she could not keep control. She was too anxious to be in situations where she felt a loss of control. This meant that she avoided contact with adults in the early years setting she attended, in case they took away her feeling of control and made her join their activities. She gathered children around her whom she could boss about, and changed the rules if any child began to threaten her feeling of total control. This was not a healthy situation. This is the sort of situation which might lead to a child becoming a dictatorial leader of a gang.

How adults can help children who dominate the play

How could Maisie be helped? She needed an adult to join her play, do her bidding, without making her feel threatened. Once she became relaxed and confident in the relationship, the adult could help her to involve other children in her play in ways which would encourage her to understand how *they* feel.

For example, she might want to pretend to play at being a demanding customer in the shop. The adult could encourage her to include other children as customers, each with a different character. One might be fussy about how something is wrapped. One might be in a hurry. One might have children. The adult might make it fun for Maisie to try and jump the queue in the shop, and see how the other characters react.

She would still be central in the story, but the adult would be helping her to see the advantages of letting other children contribute their play ideas. It would mean that the play scenario could develop a better story than it would have done. Once, over time, Maisie begins to realise this, she will begin to include the play agendas of other children. Instead of using other children to fulfill her play ideas, she will move into co-operative play. Co-operative play means she will help each child in the play to bring their ideas and feelings. They will then develop the storyline together.

The adult participation in Maisie's play creates an appropriate stepping stone towards an early learning goal.

Early Learning Goal

Personal, social and emotional development

QCA, 2000:34

Have a developing awareness of their own needs, views and feelings and be sensitive to the needs, views and feelings of others.

Notice that the way Maisie is working towards this goal is quite different from the way the newcomer is doing so (see page 101).

Key

Different children need different stepping stones towards the same goal.

(Bruce, 2000)

Summary

Well-planned play helps children to:

■ become more aware of others

■ become more sensitive towards others

■ understand how others feel (empathy)

■ realise that other people have good ideas (theory of mind)

■ recognise that their ideas might be similar to yours (theory of mind)

■ understand that their ideas might be different to yours (theory of mind)

■ find ways of using other people's ideas to make the play flow better (leadership and management)

In short, play helps children to understand other people.

8 Play is the highest form of learning in early childhood

It is in their play that children show their intelligence at the highest level of which they are capable. Play opens up new possibilities in thinking and develops the emotional intelligence that makes feelings manageable. It helps a sense of self and relationships with others to deepen.

> **Key**
>
> *Play enlarges the child's life, so that the child makes more of it.*

Play takes children out of themselves

Play helps children to explore the world beyond what they are and what they know.

- It brings spiritual awareness, by helping children to understand themselves, others and matters of the universe.

- It encourages imagination and creativity.

- It helps children to become symbol-users.

- It helps children to develop deeper and deeper layers in their use of symbols, both of their own and of others.

- It develops abstract thinking, which goes beyond the here and now into the past, future and alternative worlds.

Play takes children out of themselves, so that they can think of others in ways which are deeply caring. Froebel believed that play lifted children to their highest levels of spiritual awareness. In modern terms, this means that play helps children to know themselves, others and relate to the universe they inhabit.

112

PLAY AND CREATIVITY

Isadora Duncan (1930) was a creative dancer who innovated new techniques that changed the face of Western dance forever.

> *Isadora Duncan commented, ❝I wonder how many adults realise that by the so-called education they are giving their children, they are only driving them into the commonplace, and depriving them of any chance of doing anything beautiful or original.❞*

The world, if it is to survive, needs people who have vision, who have the imagination to see how things could be developed, improved, made better – and the creativity to make his happen. Free-flow play helps children to develop this state of mind, because it helps them to develop a feeling of control over the frightening and stressful aspects of life, as well as giving them opportunities to experiment with different ways of living and different strategies for doing things.

Free-flow play encourages us to get out of ourselves, onto a higher plane. It is difficult to describe what it feels like to be creative. Creating a dance in childhood play is a *feeling* as much as it is an *idea*. Most of the dance-like play young children engage in vanishes and fades as the play episode finishes, never to be repeated exactly. But it leaves behind traces that stay and linger in the mind. Later in life, these might be taken up and adult dances might be choreographed. Music might be composed. Dramatic plays might be written. Jazz might be improvised. Poetry might be written. A scientific invention or theory might be made.

> *This is how, in the film, 12-year-old Billy Elliot describes what it feels like to make up a dance:*
> ❝*... it sort of feels good ... once I get going I forget everything ... I start to disappear. I can feel a change in my whole body, like there's a fire in my body ... just there ... a fire ... like a bird ... electricity ... yes, like electricity ...*❞

Human beings are the only animals to develop symbolic behaviour in such depth and range. It is, therefore, desirable not to constrain children in the development towards deeper and deeper layering of symbolic behaviour (Gardner, 1983).

Humans have the possibility of becoming competent, versatile, imaginative and creative symbol-users. This means that the anxieties and dangers that are inherent parts of being creative, but which are part of improving the world, can be eased through the laughter and cathartic experiences that become possible as childhood play gradually turns into adult creativity.

WIDENING THE WORLD

Adults working with other people's children will open up the thinking of the children they spend time with, if they embrace diversity in play and value it beyond the Western European cultural heritage and tradition (Bruce and Meggitt, 1999). Part of becoming a broad-minded and deep thinker involves appreciation of the symbolic behaviour of other cultures. In this way, children learn to see that to privilege the dominant Western European culture of the UK makes their lives narrower and culturally impoverished. Children growing up in a trans-global world will need diverse ways to become flexible, adaptive and creative symbol-users. Play can make a huge contribution to this broadening process.

Learning to write

ENRICHING THE EXPERIENCE THROUGH PLAY

When children play at writing, they treat it as a problem-solving adventure. This is the approach that we will use here, as well as the way of most countries in the world. Encouraging play with writing might seem to take longer and even to waste time, but taking a long-term view it leads to steady and lasting progress. Children are offered plenty of opportunities to try things out, to explore, experiment, manipulate and discover the potential possibilities of pencils, scissors, glue and paper. Children are not rushed through their childhood; this is not a fast-track approach. There is as much emphasis on what is being written as on how it is written or how good the writing looks. It takes much longer to learn to write this way but, in the long run, it is more likely to turn children into enthusiastic writers and bookworms (Sharp and Hutchison, 1997).

Jake, the boy in the next set of photographs is playing with paper, and with pencils, a pencil case, and scissors. He is given all the time he wants and he takes two hours, supported by his mother.

▲ Playing with paper, scissors, pencils and pens.

WRITING IS PART OF A WIDER KIND OF LEARNING

Malaguzzi (1996), the Italian educator, wrote about the 'hundred languages of the child'. Learning to write is just one part of becoming a symbol-user when children are encouraged to learn writing through play. Children learn to see writing as an important way of making one thing (the symbol) stand for another. But, because of their play, they realise that writing is not the only way.

Dance, music, and mathematical symbols (such as numbers and geometric shapes) are just as important as writing. This approach to learning to write (and read) values the arts and the sciences, because they *enrich* how people write and read.

The mechanics of learning to write and read should not dominate the learning. This destroys deep learning. The story that is being written, or the story that is being read, matter more than how to form a letter or the correct spelling, at least when young children are first beginning to take the stories they have played or have listened to and put them down on paper.

Let's look at what this means for Jake.

Learning to write is hard to do. Having time to play with every element involved in writing makes it deeply satisfying, so that the motivation to write lasts across the years and throughout life.

The boy in the photographs, Jake, has made a drawing on the paper. It is a car. He seems to be pleased with it. Vygotsky (1978) says that the drawings children do are the beginnings of their writing. Gradually, they put letter-like shapes into the drawing, which they then begin to move to the edge. They put these emergent letter shapes into rows, perhaps across the top of the page. Some of the letters look like real letters. Some do not. Or, they might draw rows of zig-zag lines to represent writing. This boy is rather young yet to be making emergent letters, but his joy in drawing is already there.

He is, just as Malaguzzi suggests, exploring different ways of becoming a symbol-user. Drawing (which will turn into writing) is one way. He also wants to use the scissors. He is making use of two kinds of symbolic tool: the pencil and the scissors.

It is not easy to use a pencil or scissors when you are three years old. He needs his mother to be near him as he plays with the paper. Every so often, he hums in a satisfied way to himself.

He begins by cutting up his drawing. After all, he created it, so if he chooses to destroy it, that is fine. But is he destroying it? Every time he has cut a piece off, he holds it against the paper to make it whole again. It is a bit like a jigsaw. He seems to be playing with the idea of the whole and the parts. Children understand this concept by the time they are seven or eight years old, but they begin to explore it long before then.

He potters about. He is rarely still or in one place. He is on the move, selecting pieces of paper to cut. It might look as if he is aimless, but play does not have a definite purpose. It takes him where he didn't know he was going. It takes him where he didn't know he *could* go. It takes him out of himself, and onto a higher plane.

From time to time, in order to play at the highest level, Jake needs his mother's support. She holds the paper taut, so that he can use his latest and best cutting skills. She moves carefully, so as to give him maximum help without undermining him. He feels very good about it, and is pleased with his cutting. He is not interested in producing a finished result. This is because play is a process. It is not concerned with products. It cannot be pinned down into an end result. That is why it is called free-flow play.

USING THE 12 FEATURES OF PLAY IN THE ANALYSIS

Key

The 12 features of play

1. *Using first-hand experiences*
2. *Making up rules*
3. *Making props*
4. *Choosing to play*
5. *Rehearsing the future*
6. *Pretending*
7. *Playing alone*
8. *Playing together*
9. *Having a personal agenda*
10. *Being deeply involved*
11. *Trying out recent learning*
12. *Co-ordinating ideas, feelings and relationships for free-flow play*

(Adapted from Bruce 1991, 1996)

Again, we can see most of the features of play.

■ He is using what he knows about paper. It can be written on, or cut up. (Feature 1.)

■ He is making up sequences of cutting and replacing, considering the whole and the part. They are his own rules, which will last only whilst he plays. When the play fades, the rules will fade with it. (Feature 2.)

■ His play props are paper, pencils and scissors. (Feature 3.)

■ He has chosen to do this quite spontaneously. (Feature 4.)

■ He is rehearsing becoming a writing later in life. (Feature 5.)

■ He is playing alone, but supported by his mother. (Feature 7.)

■ He has a strong play agenda of his own. (Feature 9.)

■ He is wallowing in his play, often humming and smiling to himself. (Feature 10.)

■ He is using his latest learning, in drawing and cutting. (Feature 11.)

■ He is bringing together everything he knows about paper. (Feature 12.)

Jake's free-flow play does not use role play or pretend play on this occasion, but it is rich play none the less.

Relaxing after play

Jake is given all the time he wants for his play, and he needs two hours. At the end of his play, he is tired, because he has been wallowing very deeply. Children who dive deep in their play emerge very tired and need to be helped into a gentler, more relaxed pace.

Play is not the same as recreation. Recreation is what you do after a hard day's play! Recreation is when children relax and switch off from deep thinking. Recreation is about having fun, whereas play is about serious thinking, which might be deeply enjoyable, but which could be quite painful. Play therapy can help children to deal with sadness and pain. However, as Anna Freud knew, for most children the day-to-day play that they engage in quite naturally enables them to cope with life, and get things under control.

Making a narrative

Now let's look at the girl in these photographs.
Her name is Abigail.

▲ Exploring the potential of a box.

▲ Making a den.　　　　　　　　　▲ Supported by her mother.

In Chapter 2 we looked at the work of Lilli Nielsen, who believes that children benefit from playing in the dens that they make. When children cannot make their own dens due to a disability, she builds their own 'Little Room' around them, so that they can have this experience. She observes the child carefully, and makes a house which is based on things that interest the child. She hopes that this will be a place the child enjoys, and which, through play, opens up their learning.

Abigail's cultural context

Abigail is able to make her own play dens, and does so often. She sometimes makes dens with her friends, sometimes with her mother, and sometimes she plays alone. Her parents are very musical, and her older brother and sister also play musical instruments. Drama and dance are deeply valued, and so is using the computer. The whole family enjoys literacy and maths games using the computer, although Abigail does not use the computer yet.

Making a den – the first step to a story

On this occasion, Abigail chooses to make a den out of a cardboard box. Abigail is very imaginative in her play. The cardboard box seems to provide her with a way of creating a story in her play scenario. She needs the box as a prop to get her started.

At first, she goes in and out of the box, and experiments with it, supported in this by her mother. The mood is one of play, but she isn't yet free flowing. She's limbering up, ready to flow!

It is very important, at this point, for an adult to let her take the lead and to tune in with what she is doing, because she is sorting out a few ideas which she will then begin to use in her play. Dancers, musicians, actors and actresses, sportsmen and women and scientists all need to have time like this to prepare their thoughts and feelings in their heads, and to get their bodies ready before they can move into their highest level of functioning. Being disturbed during this time will probably mean that the moment is lost and the deep free-flow play (or the dance, piece of music, scientific invention or win of the running race) never develops. High-level play is a fragile thing. It is easily damaged before it gets under way, if the atmosphere does not help it along.

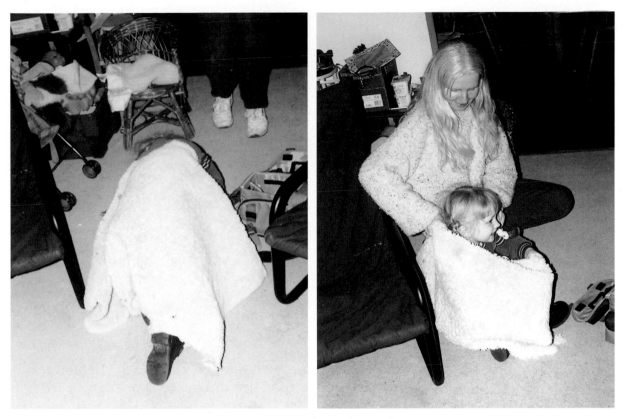

▲ Being a sheep – free-flow play with an open prop.

During the play, Abigail's mother tells her how, when she was young, she used to pretend she was a sheep. Then she puts the sheep skin rug over Abigail who likes this idea, and does just that. Adults often begin to remember the play they enjoyed during *their* childhood, as they play with young children. It creates a feeling of togetherness between the adult and the child, as we see here.

Abigail has the right atmosphere for play. She has props which are open enough to allow her play ideas. She has a place to play, and people who help her to play and who make time for it to develop without interruption. She begins to free-flow play, using the sheep-skin rug as a way of pretending to be a sheep. From this, she moves into creating a play scenario with a story and characters.

The lion in the photographs on page 122 is called Jesus. (It is Christmas time, and Abigail is brought up as a Christian). The lion Jesus and the Princess are going to get married. The Princess

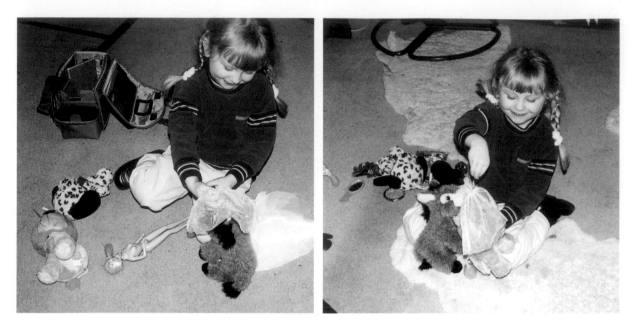

▲ Creating a story.

is preparing herself for the Ball, but gets there late. The lion Jesus marries the donkey. One of Jesus's disciples (Dalmatian) marries the Princess.

When we imagine, we use our past experiences. We rearrange them in new and fascinating ways. That is exactly what Abigail is doing in her play scenario. Several of the stories she has been told or read have been rearranged in new and fascinating ways.

The stories Abigail has used in her play scenario are:

■ Cinderella

■ Stories of Jesus

■ Stories of the disciples

■ The Lion King

■ One Hundred and One Dalmatians

The Barbie doll becomes the Princess character, and this is influenced by the story of Cinderella. In the fairy tale, Cinderella is late for the Ball. So is this character, but Abigail has rearranged the story in a new and fascinating way. The soft toys, donkey and dog need characters, so she gives them names from literature and cartoons she knows about, and incorporates them into the play scenario.

This all results in a rich play scenario. It has a story, and clearly

▲ Developing the story.

developed characters. The story has a beginning, middle and end. It takes a dramatic turn or two, but ends happily.

All of the 12 features of play are involved, especially the props and pretend play. Later, when she begins to write, Abigail will be able to pin down her stories and become a creative story writer. This should develop richly by middle childhood, when she is in junior school. But now, she is able to play out the stories she makes with great creativity and enjoyment.

Her pleasure is intense as she plays. So is her concentration and involvement in her play scenario. The ideas she has are not all happy ones. She may be exploring ideas that worry her.

Many famous people have looked back on their childhood play, and have realised how it helped them in later life.

- Richard Feynman, the scientist, had a cart and he liked to put a ball in it. He loved to watch the way the ball rolled about when he moved his cart in different ways as he played. He later studied the way atoms and electrons move about.

- Nelson Mandela remembers playing with friends in the village, on a donkey. He fell off, and the children laughed at him. He thought to himself that he would not want to humiliate people when he grew up.

- The Bronte children, Charlotte, Branwell, Emily and Anne, played with lead soldiers. As they reached middle childhood, they began to write down the stories that emerged during their play scenarios, in tiny booklets which they made. These can be seen in the Bronte Museum in Haworth, Yorkshire.

Key

When we see children beginning to move into play, we can help it along. It will be worth it, as then they will be able to move into their deepest learning. They will use this as a resource as they grow into adults.

Summary

Play helps children to function at the deepest and most wide-ranging levels they can manage.

It is not so much about learning new things, although that is one aspect of it. It is mainly about bringing together, co-ordinating and applying what has been learnt, usually with great effect and success.

If children never feel successful as learners, they will avoid deep learning. Children have to feel that the effort of learning brings some satisfaction. Play helps this to come about. Then they become learners for life, which the children we have observed in this book look all set to do.

Key messages about learning through play

BRINGING TOGETHER THREE STRANDS

This book has brought together three strands which are important when exploring the importance of play in early childhood. These are

1. the traditional view, arising out of the work of late nineteenth- and early twentieth-century pioneers of the early childhood curriculum in the UK, that play is of central importance in helping children to learn

2. evidence of a modern kind, that play supports and extends children in their learning, especially when it is well-planned

3. the QCA (2000) *Curriculum Guidance for the Foundation Stage* in the English cultural context only.

The first two strands help practitioners in the UK and wider world to develop well-planned play, in the home or group setting, as childminders, parents, or staff working in a group. The third strand gives specific help to those working in England only. In this way, practitioners, wherever they are working, can feel that they are connected to other colleagues, and are not working in isolation.

This is especially important for reception class teachers in England, or staff who do not yet feel they have sufficient training to be confident in their practice. The three strands help us to look at play so that we can all become more informed about its contribution to learning in early childhood.

Fair play in early childhood practice

Play is complex to understand and it various enormously:

■ in different cultures

■ when children have special needs or disabilities

■ for boys and girls

■ in different families

■ with different personalities.

The possibility to play is biologically within every child, but not all children will play.

The right to play is now recognised in the International Charter of Human Rights, Article 44. Play is different from *recreation* and *relaxation*, which children also need when they have been playing hard.

Fair play for early childhood practice means we need to try and find out more about common features in play because these are part of being a human. We need to explore differences that we can celebrate because they enrich the world.

Observing and describing play

THE IMPORTANCE OF OBSERVATION

Key

In order to increase our knowledge of play, and to develop practice wisdom, we need to become skilled and effective observers of play.

Observation begins with description, and then uses theory and research to analyse and interpret. In this book, the 12 features of play (Bruce, 1991) are used as a window on play, giving us a structure for interpretation. These features have emerged from the work of the pioneers of the early childhood curriculum and recent research and theory.

Observation helps us to become more informed about play. It should deepen our respect, admiration and enjoyment of the way babies, toddlers and young children learn. It should open up our thinking, and never be used to control children's play and learning.

How play makes sense of learning

Play helps children to develop their intelligence in every way.

- It helps children to think through ideas and apply them in all sorts of ways, safely in the world of play.

- It allows children to explore, manage deal with and control their feelings.

- It encourages children to develop relationships, with their inner selves, others and their universe.

- It is a biological possibility, but it is 'triggered' by people.

- It creates an attitude of mind which brings deep involvement in learning, fosters the desire to learn and to be an adventurous learner.

How play helps develop abstract ideas

MOVING FROM THE PRESENT TO THE FUTURE AND PAST

As they develop a sense of who they are (identity) and how they are different from other people (theory of mind), children begin to talk or sign and the images in their minds become more mobile. This means that, instead of thinking and feeling in the here and now, they can become increasingly abstract in the way they think, feel and relate to people, events and ideas.

This is because abstract thinking opens up possibilities of thinking backwards and forwards.

Observing, supporting and extending play

Children need places to play, objects and materials to play openly with, time to play, and, most important, people who help them to play.

Well-planned play leads practitioners to support and extend children's play through their teaching – a powerful way of helping children learn in early childhood.

Play helps children to make good use of their learning, so that they can use what they know to learn more.

127

How play helps children to understand other people

In their play, children become more aware of how other people think, feel and relate to each other. They become more sensitive to others, and to develop empathy (imagining what someone else feels or thinks). Play helps children to work out why and how people think differently from them, as they try out different ways of doing things. Play is a safe way to explore hurting, being hurt, angry, or sad, or spreading enjoyment.

Play is the highest form of learning in early childhood

When children free-flow play, alone or with others, they are able to reach their deepest and most wide-ranging levels of learning. They can do their best learning. Learning is only partly about learning *new* things. It is mainly about using what is *already known*, in flexible and imaginative ways. A child at play can do this to the full.

Putting what we know into practice

WHAT CAN PRACTITIONERS DO?

- Enjoy reading or telling stories and poems to children, and singing songs and rhymes with them.

- Play music and watch dances, so that children have ideas about what different kinds of music sound like and realise that there are many ways to dance.

- Make music and dance with children, even if you don't think you can! The adults in this book danced about in the park, kicking leaves in the autumn. This is the basis of rhythm and dance.

- Enjoy looking at nature, and objects and materials together, so that you talk about how things work, animals and the natural world.

- Value the ideas, thoughts and feelings that children have.

- Be relaxed. All of this is indirect teaching of the kind which lasts for life. The learning the children do will be used by them in their play.

- Give children plenty of time for their play.

- Join in, but don't dominate.

- Set up a challenging and exciting environment for play. Visit the park. Play in the garden, and create play scenarios indoors too.

- Make dens.

- Develop a workshop area, with everything anyone could need for drawing and writing, painting, clay, dough, and construction from found materials and wooden blocks.

- Know when to leave children to develop their own play. Children need personal space, so that they can reflect on what they know, and have the chance to understand how they think and feel, and relate to people.

- Of course, the possibilities for play are limitless, but they should be informed by the children's own interests.

Key

Don't rush children through their childhood.

A childhood that opens up play helps deep, thorough and wide-ranging learning to develop in ways which will turn into lifelong learning.

Introductory reading

Blakemore, C. Experiments worth repeating. Nursery World, 24th September, 1998

Bruce, T. (1996) Helping Young Children to Play. Hodder & Stoughton: London

Bruce, T. (1996) Tuning into Children. BBC: London

Bruce, T. and Meggitt, C. (1999, 2nd ed.) Childcare and Education. Hodder & Stoughton: London

Bruce, T. Early Learning goals: Hit for Six. Nursery World. 6th January, 2000

Gopnik, A., Meltzoff, A. and Kuhl, P. (1999) How Babies Think. Weidenfeld and Nicolson: London

Gura, P. (1996) Resources for Early Learning: Children, Adults and Stuff. Hodder & Stoughton: London

Leach, P. (1997, 3rd ed.) Your Baby and Child: The Essential Guide for Every Parent. Penguin Books: Harmondsworth

POST Report 140 (2000) Early Years Learning. The Parliamentary Office of Science and Technology

Siraj-Blatchford, I. (1994) The Early Years: Laying the Foundations for Racial Equality. Trentham Books: Stoke-on-Trent

Stoppard, M. (1995) Complete Baby and Childcare. Dorling Kindersley: London

VIDEOS

BBC/NCB (1996–1999) Tuning into children. Video and audiotapes. Available from Box 20, Tonbridge, TN12 6WU

BBC, (5/10/1998) Early Education. Panorama

Billy Elliot. (2000) A Film by Polydor

Channel 4 (29/1/1998) Too Much Too Soon. Dispatches.

Community Playthings. (1999) Blockplay in the Foundation Years. Robertsbridge, East Sussex

National Children's Bureau, (1997) Babies Communicating in the First Year.

Further reading

Athey, C. (1990) Extending Thought in Young Children: A Parent–Teacher Partnership. Paul Chapman Publishing: London

Blakemore, C. The Development of the Brain. Unpublished Lecture given at the Pen Green Conference, November, 1998

Blakemore, C. The Implications of Brain Studies for the Early Childhood Curriculum. Unpublished Lecture given at the RSA, 14th February, 2001.

Bowerman, M. (1999) Learning How to Structure Space for Language: A Cross-linguistic Perspective. In P. Bloom, M.A. Peterson, L. Nadel, M.F. Garrett (eds.) Language and Space. MIT: Cambridge, MA

Bruce, T. (1991) Time to Play in Early Childhood Education. Hodder & Stoughton: London

Bruce, T. (2000) What do brain studies tell us about how to develop a curriculum of quality for young children? Early Childhood Practice: the Journal for Multi-Professional Partnerships, vol. 2, no. 1, pp. 60–75

Calvin, W. (1997) How Brains Think. Weidenfeld and Nicolson: London

Carter, R. (1998) Mapping the Mind. Weidenfeld and Nicolson: London

Corsaro, W. (1979) We're friends, right? Children's use of access rituals in a nursery school. Language in Society, 8, pp. 315–336

Dahlberg, G., Moss, P. and Pence, A. (1999) Beyond Quality in Early Childhood Education and Care: Postmodern Perspectives. Falmer Press: London

Davies, M. (1995) Helping Children to Learn Through a Movement Perspective. Hodder & Stoughton: London

Duncan, I. (1928) My Life. Victor Gollancz: London

Dunn, J. (1988) The Beginnings of Social Understanding. Blackwell: Oxford

Dunn, J. (1991) Young Children's Understanding of Other People: Evidence from Observations Within the Family. In K. Fye and C. Moore (eds.) Theories of Mind. Lawrence Erlbaum: Hillsdale, N.J.

Feynman, R. (1990) What Do You Care What Other People Think? Further Adventures of a Curious Character. Unwin Hyman: London

Fleer, M. (1995) Staff–Child Interactions. Canberra: Australian Early Childhood Association Inc.

Gardner, H. (1993, 2nd ed.) Frames of Mind. Fontana/Harper Collins: London

Goddard-Blythe, S. First steps to the most important ABC. TES, 7, 2000

Goldschmied, E. and Jackson, S. (1994) People Under Three. Routledge: London

Haggerty, M. (1997) Using video to Work with Te Whaariki: The Experience of Five Early Childhood Centres. Wellington College of Education: New Zealand

Holland, P. (1999) Is 'Zero Tolerance' intolerance? An under-fives centre takes a fresh look at their policy on war, weapons and super hero play. Early Childhood Practice: The Journal for Multi-Professional Partnerships, vol. 1, no. 1, pp. 65–73

Isaacs, S. (1930) Intellectual Growth in Young Children. Routledge and Kegan Paul: London

Isaacs, S. (1933) Social Development in Young Children. Routledge and Kegan Paul: London

MacNaughton (2000) Rethinking Gender in Early Childhood Education. Paul Chapman Publishing: London

Malaguzzi, L. (1996) The One Hundred Languages of Children: the Exhibit. Reggio Children: Italy.

Mandler, J. (1999) Preverbal Representation and Language. In P. Boom, M.A. Peterson, L. Nadel, and M.F. Garrett, (eds.) Language and Space. MIT: Cambridge, MA

May, H. (2000) 'Mapping' some landscapes of colonial global childhood. Unpublished keynote address at the 10th Conference of the European Early Childhood Research Association on Quality of Early Childhood Education. London, August 29–September 1.

Mckellar, P. (1957) Imagination and Thinking. Cohen and West: London

Moyles, J. (ed.) (1994) The Excellence of Play. Open University: Buckingham, Philadelphia

Nielsen, L. (1992) Space and Self: Active Learning by Means of the Little Room. Sikon (Available from RNIB, National Education Centre, Garrow House, 190, Kensal Road, London, W10 5BT)

Orr, R. (2000) Fellow Travellers. Early Childhood Practice: The Journal for Multi-Professional Practice, vol. 2, no. 1, pp. 75–83

Piaget, J. (1962) Play, Dreams and Imitation in Childhood. Routledge and Kegan Paul: London

Rice, S. (1998) Luke's Story. In J. Dwyfor Davies, P. Gamer and J. Lee, (eds.) Managing Special Needs in Mainstream Schools: the Role of the SENCO. David Fulton Publishers: London

RNIB (1995) Play it My Way. HMSO: London

Rogoff, B., Mosier, B., Mistry, J. and Goncu, A., (1998) Toddlers' Guided Participation with their Caregivers in Cultural Activity. In M. Woodhead, D. Faulkner and K. Littleton (eds.) Cultural Worlds of Early Childhood. Routledge in association with the Open University: London, New York

Sharp, C. and Hutchison, D. (1997) How do Season of Birth and Length of Schooling Affect Children's Attainment at Keystage 1? A Question Revisited. NFER: Slough

Talmy, L. (1999) Fictive Motion in Language and 'ception', in P. Bloom, M.A. Peterson, L. Nadel, and M.F. Garrett, Language and Space. MIT: Cambridge, MA

Trevarthen, C. (1998) The Child's Need to Learn a Culture. In M. Woodhead, D. Faulkner and K. Littleton, (eds.) Cultural Worlds of Early Childhood. Routledge: London

United Nations Convention (1990) The Rights of the Child

Vygotsky, L. (1978) Mind in Society: the Development of Higher Psychological Processes. Harvard University Press: Cambridge, MA

Whalley, M. (1994) Learning to be Strong: Setting Up a Neighbourhood Service for Under-Fives and Their Families. Hodder & Stoughton: London

Whalley, M. (ed.) (2000) Involving Parents in their Children's Learning. Paul Chapman Publishing: London

Index